Be ready to give a defense of

the hope that is within you.

THE APOSTLE PETER

A Little Primer on Humble Apologetics

JAMES W. SIRE

IVP Books

An imprint of InterVarsity Press
Downers Grove, Illinois

InterVarsity Press
P.O. Box 1400, Downers Grove, IL 60515-1426
World Wide Web: www.ivpress.com
E-mail: email@ivpress.com

InterVarsity Press® is the book-publishing division of InterVarsity Christian Fellowship/USA®, a student movement active on campus at hundreds of universities, colleges and schools of nursing in the United States of America, and a member movement of the International Fellowship of Evangelical Students. For information about local and regional activities, write Public Relations Dept., InterVarsity Christian Fellowship/USA, 6400 Schroeder Rd., P.O. Box 7895, Madison, WI 53707-7895, or visit the IVCF website at <www.intervarsity.org>.

Scripture quotations, unless otherwise noted, are from the New Revised Standard Version of the Bible, copyright 1989 by the Division of Christian Education of the National Council of the Churches of Christ in the USA. Used by permission. All rights reserved.

Design: Cindy Kiple

Images: Digital Vision/Getty Images

ISBN-10: 0-8308-3382-X
ISBN-13: 978-0-8308-3382-5

Printed in the United States of America ∞

Library of Congress Cataloging-in-Publication Data

Sire, James W.
  A little primer on humble apologetics / James W. Sire.
    p. cm.
  Includes bibliographical references and index.
  ISBN-13: 978-0-8308-3382-5 (pbk.: alk. paper)
  ISBN-10: 0-8308-3382-X (pbk.: alk. paper)
  1. Apologetics. I. Title.
  BT1103.S57 2006
  239—dc22
                                                                        2006013526

P	19	18	17	16	15	14	13	12	11	10	9	8	7	6	5	4	3	2	1
Y	21	20	19	18	17	16	15	14	13	12	11	10	09	08	07	06				

To Francis Schaeffer

(in memoriam)

Contents

Preface

THE MOMENT THE CHURCH was born, apologetics was born with it. The wind of the Spirit stirred the disciples gathered at Pentecost, and the believers broke out in strange languages that both excited and baffled them. Then Peter stood and spoke, explaining what was happening. He was, shall we say, the first Christian apologist.

That was long ago and far away; Peter was an apostle, the emerging leader of the fledgling church. Still, here we are. Each of us has met Jesus in the Scriptures, in the lives of our friends, and in the heart of our heart as we commune with him in prayer. We recapitulate in our own lives the early church. We know Jesus, and we want to communicate his reality to a confused and troubled world.

What can we learn from the early apostles—from Peter, Steven, Paul and the writers of the Gospels? How can we make an effective case for the Christian faith? What is it exactly that we are to do? How can we do it well?

The present book is indeed what its title says—a *primer,* a very first book exploring the nature of Christian apologetics, which, simply defined, is a *defense* of the Christian faith. So chapter one opens by looking at what nine key New Testament passages say about presenting the gospel, and it finally arrives at a definition that can guide us in our witness. Then, because of frequent distortions of apologetic theory and practice, we turn in the next two chapters to the values and the limits of apologetics. Chapter four examines the various audiences Christians may address—formal ones in public presentations, more informal small groups and casual one-on-one conversations. Chapter five delineates five positive arguments for the Christian faith and responses to five objections to the Christian faith; it then suggests books that can help flesh out these arguments. Finally, for those readers who are drawn to apologetics as a lifestyle, chapter six considers how we might discern God's call to life as an apologist.

This book is, of course, only a primer. So one of its primary intents is to encourage further reading, study and—most of all—practice. Christian apologetics, born with the early church, will disappear only when the reality of Christ crucified, buried and resurrected is fulfilled in the coming fullness of the kingdom of God. In the mean time we have work to do.

I cannot acknowledge the contributions of the countless people who have somehow influenced the writing of this book: my mentors and predecessors in the school of apologetics, my colleagues in Inter-Varsity Christian Fellowship and the International Fellowship of Evangelical Students, my students in a variety of colleges, universities and seminaries, and those who have sat through my apologetic sessions and, even if they were not convinced, let me get away without being stoned. But a few certainly deserve mention. First is Francis A. Schaeffer, who was not just a mentor but a friend and model for intellectual and personal apologetics. This book is dedicated to his memory. Then come philosophers Paul Chamberlain and Douglas Groothuis, who read the manuscript and offered good advice. Longtime colleague and editor Jim Hoover helped inspire the shape of the book, and Ruth Goring, with a keen sense for detail, polished the prose. My thanks go to all of them. The remaining gaffes and infelicities are my own.

The Scope of
Christian Apologetics

AN AMERICAN IN Swiss lederhosen stands at the podium of a large university auditorium in New England. The students filling the seats are facing the Vietnam draft and what they see as arrogant American aggression in Southeast Asia. Instead of poring over their standard textbooks and writing their assigned papers, they have been devouring the works of Karl Marx and Friedrich Nietzsche, Herbert Marcuse and Franz Fanon, Jean-Paul Sartre and Albert Camus. Instead of pouring acid into water in their chemistry labs and measuring the rise in temperature, they have been engaging in campus protests, threatening to take over buildings and shut down the administration. What will go on for the next couple of hours, however, will be brilliant apologetics geared precisely to the character and temperament of these angry and often despairing students.[1]

In a top research university in Chicago, a radical theologian and an evangelical historian face off in a debate over whether God is dead.[2]

An obscure British literary scholar, veteran of World War I, speaks over BBC radio to an audience whose country is again involved in a world war, discussing the viability of Christian faith in a world stricken with violent conflict. Later these lectures become the twentieth century's most read intellectual defense of "mere" Christianity.[3]

A young British cleric sits at his desk and pens a clear exposition of the nature and character of Jesus and his role in setting humanity free from the guilt of sin. The result is one of the clearest explanations of why one should place faith in this Jesus, the very Son of God.[4]

In the past fifty years, tens of thousands of Christian students all over the world have repeated and elaborated on the arguments of such apologists as these. Just what is it that all these people have in common? What is apologetics? We will begin with the view of the New Testament, the ultimate source of all good apologetics, and then take up both the values and limits of apologetics in the modern world.

What Is Apologetics?

DEFINITIONS OF APOLOGETICS range from highly specific and focused to general and vague. As will gradually become plain, my approach is closer to the latter than the former. Apologetics involves relationships, lots of them. There are, of course, the human relationships between the apologist and the audience (one or many); between individual people in the audience; between the apologist, the audience and their (same or different) social contexts. But there are also the divine relationships between God and the apologist, God and the audience, and God and the social context in which the other human and divine relationships are embedded.

Academic apologetics that focus primarily on largely abstract intellectual arguments for the Christian faith often fail when they are placed in the context of living human beings. Effective, practical apologetics involves the whole panorama of divine and human relationships. It takes place in the realm of human thought and emotion, which, though permeated by the presence of the Holy Spirit, limit its ability to establish once and for all the claims of Christianity.

How we define *apologetics* will, then, necessarily reflect this complexity. Apologetics is both less than and more than an abstract, rationally sound demonstration of the truth of the Christian faith.[1] We need a more relational and more humble definition than this. In what follows I want to move toward that definition.

A BIBLICAL FOUNDATION

The way forward is, I believe, set before us primarily in the New Testament by the teachings and examples of Jesus and the apostles.[2]

Apologetics as response to persecution. We begin with the text most often quoted by those defining apologetics. It is, I think, the most important one. I am quoting more of the context than is usually found in books of apologetics, because I believe that the biblical context helps us understand the role of human and divine relationships in both the ancient world of the apostle Peter and our world.

In his first letter Peter, probably writing from Rome, is addressing Christians in Asia Minor. Both Peter and his audience were facing persecution, some perhaps only minor ridicule, some more severe.[3] But the response of Christians was to be the same. With each other, Christians were to "have unity of spirit, sympathy, love for one another, a tender heart, and a humble mind" (1 Pet 3:8). To the surrounding community, they were not to "repay evil for evil or abuse for abuse; but, on the contrary, repay with a blessing" (v. 9). Peter continues:

> Now who will harm you if you are eager to do what is good? But even if you do suffer for doing what is right, you are blessed. Do not fear what they fear, and do not be intimidated, but in your hearts sanctify Christ as Lord. Always be prepared to make your defense to anyone who demands from you an accounting for the hope that is in you; yet do it with gentleness and reverence. Keep your conscience clear, so that when you are maligned, those who abuse you for your good conduct in Christ may be

put to shame. For it is better to suffer for doing good, if suffering should be God's will, than to suffer for doing evil. For Christ also suffered for sins once for all, the righteous for the unrighteous, in order to bring you to God. (1 Pet 3:13-18)

In the heart of this passage is the intellectual core of apologetics. The Christians in Asia Minor are to be ready to make their defense (*apologia*) of the special hope that is theirs. But this intellectual core is set in the social situation the Christians were facing. Let us look first at the core.

In ancient Greece, *apologia* was a term associated with responding to a charge in court. In the present passage, it is unclear whether Peter had such an official context in mind. Of course, Christians were sometimes brought before the magistrates. Whether or not that was the case here, the term itself signals that a serious matter was involved. The defense that Christians would muster would involve careful consideration, probably citing evidence defending against untrue charges and favoring their specific "hope"—their fundamental attitude toward life in the present and the future. One can only speculate as to what evidence might be relevant. That would depend on the specific charges and on what aspect of Christian hope was challenged.

Several aspects of the context are important. First, persecution made Christian defense necessary. Four times in his letter Peter refers to suffering for the faith (1:6-7; 3:13-17; 4:12-19; 5:9). The first two assume mild persecution; the second two assume abuse and an imminent "fiery ordeal." What they were being accused of is unclear, but it was something to which their neighbors or, perhaps, the government objected. So they were forced to respond. Their natural response would have been to "repay evil with evil," but instead Peter in no uncertain terms tells them to "repay with a blessing" and thus let the accusers see for themselves the evil of their own ways. If necessary, they were to live the gospel by suffering as had their Lord and Savior.

Second, their defense was to be given when it was *demanded*. Apologists today would love to have people demand that they explain themselves. But these Christians were not out on an evangelistic crusade. They were quietly living their lives as Christians but attracting enough attention to cause their neighbors to wonder who they were, what they were living for and why.

Third, they were to be ready to give that defense. They were living out their faith; now they had to explain it. They had an understanding and diagnosis of human ills, they knew the remedy, and they had a hope that linked the present crisis with a transcendent future. Indeed they knew the good news of the kingdom, and Peter told them to share it.[4]

Fourth, they were to do so with "gentleness and reverence"—no browbeating, no insulting the benighted beliefs of their neighbors, only kind words to penetrate the confusion and restrain the hatred of their persecutors. In short, reason and reasons were not enough; rhetoric was to clothe the discourse so that the good, strong reasons given could be recognized and minds and hearts could be changed.

It is important to see that the core notion of apologetics—the defense of the Christian faith—is not the focus of this passage. The central concern is the presence of persecution, the likelihood of its increasing and what to do about it. Living a truly godly life—responding to evil with goodness—is Peter's focus. Rational apologetics (defense) comes in as only one aspect of that response. The emphasis is more on the character of the Christians' lives than on the explanation of their hope.

It may seem odd for a book on apologetics to make a special note of this. But it is important to see that a humble holy life (there is no unhumble holy life) is far more significant than one's ability to fashion and present a verbal apologetic for that life. The holy life of one of God's redeemed children living alone in a hostile environment is itself a strong apologetic. Even more so is a Christian community intent on living out its faith and actually doing so. If members of such a community are being persecuted and they gently give a reason for the hope that is within them, their apologetic becomes even more powerful.

Apologetics as explanation and proclamation (Acts 2:1-42). The apostle Peter himself engaged in apologetics on the day of Pentecost, when the Holy Spirit came upon the believers gathered in Jerusalem. The tongues of fire and the sudden outbreak of speech in the languages of the "devout Jews from every nation under heaven living in Jerusalem" (v. 5) caused such a commotion and attracted so much attention that Peter, surrounded by the rest of Jesus' disciples, addressed the gathering crowd. He explained what was happening, linked it to Hebrew prophecy, and then explained who it was they had just crucified, what had happened later (the resurrection) and, again by reference to the Scriptures, what it all meant.

Here apologetic proclamation emerged from events. It had not been planned by the disciples but was their response to a stellar opportunity to present the gospel in a fully intelligible and intelligent way. That day about three thousand people were added to the community of faith. Today we would call this mass evangelism. Then it was a simple, completely reasonable response under the impetus and in the presence of the Holy Spirit.

Apologetics as deliberate argument (Acts 17:1-9). Paul and Silas had been traveling through Asia Minor into Macedonia and had stopped at Thessalonica, where there was a synagogue. As Luke, the author of Acts, says, "Paul went in, as was his custom, and on three

sabbath days *argued* with them from the scriptures." The flow of
Paul's argument is well adapted to the context. First, because his audience was Jewish worshipers, his authority was the Hebrew Scriptures. Second, he needed to show that the Hebrew Scriptures taught
something these worshipers did not already believe. So he began
with an exegesis showing that it was necessary for the Messiah to suffer, die and be resurrected. This ran counter to their received notion
that the Messiah would inaugurate and rule the kingdom of God.

Then Paul identified Jesus as the Messiah. This was a notion utterly foreign to them. Nonetheless, some Jews and even some "devout Greeks" and "leading women" were persuaded. Others, however, became jealous and got a mob together to wreak havoc on Paul
and Silas and to "set the city in an uproar" (v. 5). The believers then
sent Paul and Silas on to safety in Beroea. Unlike in 1 Peter, here the
apologetic and its success preceded the persecution.

Apologetics as confrontation (Acts 17:16-34). As an apologist with
university students, I have long been fascinated by the apostle Paul's
presentation to the philosophers in Athens. My encounters with university students and teachers has usually been quite deliberate. Paul,
however, was not intent on engaging the academy. It just happened as
a normal event in the course of his life as an itinerant missionary.

Paul had fled from Thessalonica to Beroea, where he was received
by the Jews with much more sympathy. Nonetheless, Jews from
Thessalonica eventually stirred up trouble in Beroea, whereupon
Paul went on to Athens and waited for Silas and Timothy to join him.
In Athens he continued his strategy to witness from the Scriptures to
the Jews in the synagogue and more culturally to the Greeks in the
marketplace. Some philosophers became intrigued and began to argue with him. This interaction led to a full-fledged lecture in which
he made no reference to the Hebrew Scriptures but instead linked the

message of the gospel to the Greek philosophers' interest in religion, a statue to an "unknown God" and the Athenians' fascination with anything new.[5] The Greeks would not have known the Scriptures or, even if they had, would not have lent to them any credibility. Paul's approach was to draw distinctions between the gospel (and the Christian worldview in general) and the worldviews of the Epicureans, the Stoics and the Greeks in general. The reaction was again mixed: some "scoffed," some still remained curious and some became believers. Unlike the Thessalonians, however, the Athenians did not arrest or disturb Paul in any way.

This event in Athens, some believe, is the quintessential model for apologetics in a university context. I am among them.

Apologetics as humble spiritual demonstration (1 Cor 2:1-5). Paul traveled then from Athens to Corinth. Again he began with the Jewish population, arguing every sabbath in the synagogue, and sought to convince the Greeks as well. Here the Jews rejected him, and so he left the Jewish community and took up residence with Titius, a "worshiper of God" (that is, a Gentile who was attracted to Jewish belief and worship). This more neutral venue attracted both Greeks and Jews, and in the year and a half that Paul was in Corinth many became believers. Even Crispus, an official in the synagogue, and his family became Christians. Writing later from Rome, Paul talks about his apologetic approach at Corinth:

> When I came to you, brothers and sisters, I did not come proclaiming the mystery of God to you in lofty words of wisdom. For I decided to know nothing among you except Jesus Christ, and him crucified. And I came to you in weakness and in fear and in much trembling. My speech and my proclamation were not with plausible words of wisdom, but with a demonstration

of the Spirit and of power, so that your faith might rest not on human wisdom but on the power of God. (1 Cor 2:1-5)

Some people today see this comment as a rejection of his previous approach in Athens. They argue that Paul abandoned the rational apologetics of Acts 17 and replaced it with a heartfelt emotional appeal. That is possible. But it is much more likely that he was again adapting his approach to fit the new context. In Athens he came naturally in contact with the intellectuals, so he gave an intellectual response. Corinth was a busy port city on an isthmus—a major transportation route from Europe and the islands to the west to Asia Minor to the east. Prostitution, lax sexual liaisons, drunkenness, the attractions of the flesh all abounded. His message was the same, but he matched his approach to the audience.[6] The church that emerged from his time there was filled with all sorts of problems, detailed and dealt with in Paul's two letters. A discourse on philosophy was hardly appropriate in such a city.

Apologetics as personal participation (1 Cor 9:19-23). In this section of his first letter to the Corinthian church, Paul defends himself against his critics, though against precisely what charge is unclear. What is clear is Paul's insistence that he has always lived, sometimes sacrificially, so that people will be attracted to the gospel:

For though I am free with respect to all, I have made myself a slave to all, so that I might win more of them. To the Jews I became as a Jew, in order to win Jews. To those under the law I became as one under the law (though I myself am not under the law) so that I might win those under the law. To those outside the law I became as one outside the law (though I am not free from God's law but am under Christ's law) so that I might win those outside the law. To the weak I became weak, so that I might win the weak. I have become all things to all people, so that I might by all means possible save some. I do this all for the sake of the gospel.

Here is intimate, participatory, lifestyle, personally engaged apologetics. It is the gospel lived out.

Apologetics as correcting error and misbehavior (2 Cor 10:1-6; Jude 3). In preparing for an upcoming return to the church in Corinth, the apostle Paul made a direct appeal to those in the church who were holding him and his teaching in contempt. The issue Paul was addressing is unclear, but it had to do with two matters, one of temperament and one of character. First, his critics saw an inconsistency in Paul's demeanor. He seemed to be humble and even weak in their presence but bold and aggressive when he wrote them his letters. Second, they accused him of acting "according to human standards" (2 Cor 10:2). Paul was quick to respond, saying, "Indeed, we live as human beings, but we do not wage war according to human standards; for the weapons of our warfare are not merely human, but they have divine power to destroy strongholds. We destroy arguments and every proud obstacle raised up against the knowledge of God, and we take every thought captive to obey Christ" (2 Cor 10:3-5). Paul will be quite willing to exercise discipline when he arrives, if the wrongdoers' disobedience continues till then.

Of course, the immediate context of this passage is church discipline—the need to secure the Corinthian church from apostasy and misbehavior, both quite easy to come by in a church set in the heart of a pagan and dissolute seaport.[7] But the principle to which Paul appeals has a more universal application. Paul insists that what will make his actions effective is not the human strength of his character or the power of his rationality but the divine spiritual power of the truth of God himself. The proud obstacles raised against the true knowledge of God will be refuted by Paul's arguments as he makes "every thought captive to obey Christ."

Christians in the university world today often quote this phrase as they attempt to integrate their Christian faith and their academic work. The context is very different from that of Corinth. Paul was contending with those in the church; Christian academics are contending with intellectual theories that ignore or contradict or reject the notion of God or spiritual reality of any kind. But in both cases the goal is the same: to "destroy" the case against the "knowledge of God" and to "take every thought captive to obey Christ." After all, only because God is there as Creator and sustainer of the world is there a world to know, and only because God has made human beings in the image of his infinite knowledge can anyone, including university researchers and academics, know anything at all. Actually, every thought is already "captive" to Christ; it just takes the divine power of God's "weapons of warfare" to show that this is the case. And that is one role of apologetics.

The tone of the opening verses of 1 Corinthians 10 is harsher than that in the opening chapters. Here, what is at stake is a matter internal to the local congregation. Those who are misbehaving are supposed to be believers, so Paul makes a sterner response than he does to those who have yet to commit themselves to Christ. Jude, too, takes a hard, critical approach (Jude 2-4). In this both Paul and Jude are acting much like Jesus, who saved his harshest remarks for the scribes and Pharisees who thought they knew God but did not.

Apologetics as personal witness (1 Jn 1:1-4). The apostle John's first letter opens with a beautiful literary allusion to the opening of his Gospel and proceeds to turn that allusion into the foundation for his apologetic:

We declare to you what was from the beginning, what we have heard, what we have seen with our eyes, what we have looked at and touched with our hands, concerning the word of life—this life was revealed, and we have seen it and testify to it, and declare to you the eternal life that was with the Father and was revealed to us—we declare to you what we have seen and heard so that you also may have fellowship with us; and truly our fellowship is with the Father and with his Son Jesus Christ.

John declares his authority for writing: He has seen the word of life himself. Jesus was no ghost, no Gnostic disembodied spirit. Jesus the Christ was the very Word made flesh. Acceptance of the incarnation—the Word made flesh—is itself a test of a true teacher (1 Jn 4:1-3).

Of course, John is writing a pastoral letter to Christians, not making a case for Christ to those who have yet to believe. Still, his letter is an apologetic—a case for living the Christian life to the fullest, made by an aging apostle who knew Jesus up close and personal. Here is apologetics as intimate personal witness.

Apologetics as presentation of Jesus Christ as God (Jn 20:30). Apologetics is not just done by public speaking or private conversations. From the beginning, it was also done in documents. The Gospels themselves are primarily apologetic tracts. That is, their main purpose is to set forth a case for the Christian faith, a case to be made for both believers and those yet to believe. The Gospel of John is specific and direct: "Now Jesus did many other signs in the presence of his disciples, which are not written in this book. But these are written so that you may come to believe that Jesus is the Messiah, the Son of God, and that through believing you may have life in his name" (Jn 20:30).

The very rhetorical structure of John's Gospel substantiates this. The so-called prologue (Jn 1:1-18) sets forth the epistemological foundation for the argument. There are five intertwining reasons why we can know who and what God, humanity and the universe actually are. They begin with the declaration (1) that there is one God who is truly there (Being itself) and (2) that God knows all there is to know; in fact, that he is Intelligence or Meaning itself and has the capacity to express that intelligence: "In the beginning was the Word, and the Word was with God, and the Word was God" (v. 1). (3) Knowledge itself is christocentric and therefore personal: "He was in the beginning with God" (v. 2). (4) God the Word (Being and Meaning itself) created the cosmos (everything that is is either God or the cosmos), and therefore everything is meaningful. "All things came into being through him, and without him not one thing came into being" (v. 3). (5) People can know because God illumined them, gave them the capacity to know: "In him was life, and that life was the light of all people" (v. 4).

The argument of the remainder of the Gospel rests on this ontological foundation: the God Who Is There is also the God Who Knows. He has made a universe that can be known and made human beings in that universe capable of doing so as well. God made us in his image and wants us to be like him in our knowing. Of course, our knowledge is limited first by our finitude and then by our fallenness. But God still wants us to know. This, then, is the epistemological foundation not only for the remainder of this Gospel but for all human knowledge both sacred and secular, both that which comes by special revelation and that which comes by our ordinary created abilities.

The second section of the Gospel of John (1:19—12:49) tells the story of Jesus' encounters with a variety of men and women. In the early chapters, these are the people like the twelve apostles (Nathanael especially) and the woman at the well, who easily grasp that Jesus is a very special prophet and quickly become his disciples. Through her witness, her neighbors also meet Jesus and come to believe in him. Gradually, as the gospel continues, opposition grows and Jesus argues strenuously with religious leaders whom even he fails to persuade. But by the end of chapter 12, this part of Jesus' apologetic ("that you may believe that Jesus is the Christ" [20:30]) is over.

In the third section of the Gospel (13:1-17), Jesus speaks exclusively to his inner circle of followers (those who, having believed, now "have life in his name" [20:30]). Here we find the discourse in the Upper Room, in which Jesus takes his disciples deeply into the riches of spiritual life.

Section four (18:1—20:29) recounts Jesus' arrest, the final hours of his life, the crucifixion and the resurrection. These events serve as the clincher for the argument. Such a man as this is indeed the Son of God, sent by the Father to make eternal life with God possible for us.

A final section (21:1-25) concerns Jesus postresurrection teaching and propels the readers toward understanding that they live in this postresurrection world and can rest on the assurance that God will do for all his followers what he shows that he has done for his first disciples.

The Synoptic Gospels (Matthew, Mark and Luke) are not structured as arguments. But the central thrust of each is the answer to the question, Who is Jesus? And the answer the Gospels give is itself an apologetic, for the best reason for believing in a God who is worthy to be trusted with your life is Jesus himself. The Gospels witness to him, cause us to stand before him and present his demand for a decision. There is no stronger apologetic.

APOLOGETICS DEFINED

On the most basic and abstract level, then, Christian apologetics is simply the presentation of a case for biblical truth, most notably the central truth of Jesus Christ as Son of God and Savior. But a richer,

more relational and more humble definition must include the central
concern of apologetics:

> Christian apologetics lays before the watching world such
> a winsome embodiment of the Christian faith that for any
> and all who are willing to observe there will be an intel-
> lectually and emotionally credible witness to its funda-
> mental truth.

The success of any given apologetic argument is not whether it
wins converts but whether it is faithful to Jesus.[8] Both the reasons
that are given and the rhetoric that expresses these reasons must
demonstrate their truth. God uses all sorts of ill-conceived and
poorly argued presentations of the gospel. Thank God for that! But
this does not excuse us from honoring him by making our lives living
embodiments of the gospel truth—before and in, around and after,
our apologetic forays. For us as Christians acting as apologists, this is
indeed our spiritual worship (Rom 12:1).

Kent State University, April 1990

IN A CLASS CALLED Introduction to Political Thought, students had read the first seventy pages of Allan Bloom's *The Closing of the American Mind*, a book that in the late 1980s sparked controversy all over the university world. The opening sentence set the tone: "There is one thing a professor can be absolutely certain of: almost every student entering the university believes, or says he believes, that truth is relative."

After reminding the students of the essence of Bloom's argument and proposing that Christian theism would be a way out of the dilemmas posed by relativism, I opened the door for discussion. The result? Pandemonium. Well, controlled pandemonium. Students quickly took sides. "Yes," said several in different ways, "I believe there are distinct moral values, but who can decide what they are?" "Of course, there are universal rules. Everyone can and should decide them for themselves," said others. But two students' responses stood out.

One woman, responding to my proposal that Yahweh, an infinite, personal, good and all-knowing God, provides an absolute standard by which to judge right from wrong, said, "Are you trying to tell me that I should attach a value to God?" It took five minutes of dialogue to help her and the class see that the very way she formed the question indicated the depths of her own involvement in relativism.

A second woman said, with no sense of reservation, that she was having an affair with a married man. She remarked, "I'm a good person. I don't like the Ten Commandments [though she did say some were okay]. I don't see anything wrong with sleeping with a married man if it doesn't hurt anyone." And then she asked, "Are you trying to tell me I'm immoral?"

To both of these students my reply was simple. If we are to have a society that can justly arrest and convict a child molester, a wife beater or a murderer, we will have to have an objective standard. The Christian God provides one very good objective standard. We can't attach a value to him. He attaches a value to us. If he is the standard of good, then our actions—mine as well as the students'—are weighed by him, not them or me.

At the end of the class the professor reminded his students of a similar discussion a few weeks earlier and pointed out how some who were on one side of the debate had switched unwittingly to the other side. He noted that three comments from the earlier discussion still stuck in his mind. One student had maintained that "Hitler was just doing his thing." A black student said, "If it had been the blacks in Africa who had captured the European whites to work their fields in Africa, that would have been okay." A third argued that the Ayatollah Khomeini was justified in sending six-year-old Iranian children through minefields to trip the mines and thus make way for soldiers, since the ayatollah believed that these children would immediately be rewarded in heaven.

The professor, himself having some sympathy with Christian faith, was visibly disturbed by these comments and challenged the class to think hard about these matters.

The Value of Apologetics

As we saw in the previous chapter, biblical apologetics is appropriate in a variety of circumstances: during times of persecution or outbreaks of spectacular religious phenomena, and likewise when non-Christians are curious about what Christians believe or when Christians are enticed by false teaching. Apologetics can take place in synagogues, churches, city markets, places of education and cultural exchange—in short, wherever ordinary people are carrying on the business of daily life. Its form can be conversation or teaching, dialogue or written document. Its tone can range from quiet dialogue to tough, intense interchange and debate. Apologetics, in short, varies according to the situation. But in every situation effective apologetics requires reason and rhetoric to work together to support each other and thus enhance the credibility of the gospel.

Apologetics is, of course, not the solution to all problems in society and the church. It has both values and limitations.[1] In this chapter we will deal with the former.

ESTABLISHMENT OF THE FAITH FOR BELIEVERS

When Christians hear the word *apologetics*, they have either one of two reactions. Most will say, "What's that?" The term itself appears new and odd, for churches pay little attention to apologetics in Sunday school or from the pulpit. The second reaction is "Oh, you mean a philosophical argument intended to convert skeptics to the Christian faith." Few see a role for apologetics in their normal church programs. I want to counter that view. The first and most important value of apologetics is to establish Christians in their faith.

There is no time in a Christian's life when apologetics is not helpful. Take the case of Jack, a Christian raised from birth in a Christian home. Through a variety of influences, he comes to see Jesus as his Lord and Savior and matures through the ordinary disciplines of Christian faith: prayer, Bible study, worship, attendance at Sunday school. His faith is not challenged by any of his experience until he reaches fifth or sixth grade and realizes that his friends don't seem to believe what he does. Jack mentions this to his parents and his Sunday school teacher, but their response is not helpful. They say, "Don't worry about that. Different people believe different things. You're a Christian; you know what's right. Just believe what we've been teaching you." Or they may simply say, "Don't ask questions, son. There's no need to be concerned. Just believe."

What is Jack to do? He has run out of options. If he thinks at all, it will be easy for him to doubt his faith, find it growing less and less relevant to his life, and slip quietly into unbelief.[2] (Note: I do not wish to raise here the knotty question of whether a person can lose salvation. I am only describing a common phenomenon: young people often move away from the faith of their family.)

What Jack needs is exposure to simple, basic apologetics—not necessarily the sophisticated arguments one finds in the works of C. S. Lewis or Francis A. Schaeffer, but clear exposition of the essential elements of Christianity and the solid reasons that they are not only credible but true. Apologetics of this kind should begin at the lowest levels of Christian education at home and in the church. For some, of course, conscious doubts do not come till high school or even college. But modern society is so permeated with ideas and values that run counter to biblical faith that the erosion of the Christian worldview begins earlier than is usually detected by either childhood believers or their elders. Christian education at home and school is vital, not just to the preservation of childhood belief but to spiritual growth itself. There is no time at which believers should not be ready to give a solid accounting for their faith in Christ as Lord and Savior.

Valery's case is different. Her family is mostly secular. Her parents have never attended church, and when she was a child they did not even drop her off at Sunday school and pick her up later. She got interested in a boy in high school, and he invited her to his church youth group, where she learned all sorts of things that were new and surprising. At the end of a summer camp sponsored by the church, she gave her life to Jesus, as she would explain to her school friends who were not a part of the youth group. Imagine the courage she now needs to explain her conversion and to hold on to her faith in light of the disbelief of her friends and the ridicule she is sure to experience. If she has not thought through her commitment before she made it, she will have to do so now. That is, she needs a living, relevant apologetic either before she makes the commitment or immediately thereafter. When she graduates and begins to attend Desperate State University, she will need an even more sophisticated apologetic.

So long as a Christian is alive to the surrounding culture, so long will there be a need for a growing, maturing apologetic. Apologetics should be a staple subject in every church.

DEFENSE OF THE FAITH TO SKEPTICS AND SEEKERS

The most common understanding of apologetics, however, is as a respectable defense of the faith to a skeptic or seeker. There is a very close relationship between apologetics and evangelism. One could say that apologetics is simply evangelism done with the intellectual sophistication necessary for a specific situation.

The oral forums for such apologetics range from intimate one-on-one conversions and small group discussions to full public lectures. Over the past fifty years I have been involved in a host of conversations and heard or given hundreds of such lectures, primarily to university students on secular campuses in North America and Europe. I will not give any details here, but in the course of this book I will draw on this experience for illustrations of both effective approaches and some rather distressing gaffes. I trust that others can learn from my and other apologists' mistakes and take courage from the occasional successes.

Modern published examples of apologetics also abound. They range from the utterly basic to the highly sophisticated. I will mention only a very few of the more salient, leading off with the most well known. At the beginning of this list are G. K. Chesterton's *Orthodoxy* (1908) and *The Everlasting Man* (1925). The latter was a significant factor in the conversion of English literary scholar C. S. Lewis. When Lewis himself spoke out for Christian faith on BBC Radio in the 1940s, his talks were so popular that they were issued in three thin volumes and then combined. The result, *Mere Christianity* (1952), has been a milestone on the path to faith for many people, including those, like Charles Colson, who have gone on to write their own defenses of the faith. Both Chesterton and Lewis, in styles uniquely their own, combined clever rhetoric with sound reasoning and have attracted hundreds of thousands of readers. John Stott's straightforward biblical presentation of Jesus as Lord and Savior in *Basic Christianity* has likewise moved many to accept the claims of Christ. Finally, there is the work of Francis A. Schaeffer, whose *Escape from Reason* (1968) and *The God Who Is There* (1968) introduced many to Christian faith through a critique of culture. (A more extensive list of books that are especially helpful for beginning apologists will be found in chapter five of this book.)

The key to the success of each of these apologetic works is that they begin in a world common to their readers and call them to pay attention to some feature of that world that they can't deny. These features include such things as the oddness of the universe (Chesterton), the universally human sense of morality (Lewis), the astounding nature of the claims of Christ (Stott), and the presence of personality in the universe (Schaeffer). From there they show that the best explanation for what they take to be true is the Christian understanding of reality.

By no means do all people come to faith only after considering a rational argument, but no one believes what they are certain is not true. When the barrier to belief is intellectual doubt, something has to happen to break the barrier. That is a major distinctive role of apologetics.

A Heightened Understanding of Our Culture

Apologetics if it is to be done well, demands a heightened understanding of our culture. This, of course, is no small thing. In the United States and many other societies it is easy to go through life as a believer, enjoying the comforts of the security Christian faith affords. After all, while we are not promised the proverbial rose garden, we do receive countless benefits from our Christian community: a sense of belonging, a feeling that we are headed in the right direction, a lot of support from friends when we hit the hard spots. We can get these benefits without strenuous intellectual effort, often without doing much of anything at all. Our spiritual life may not grow or prosper much, but we may not notice.

Once we begin to talk about our faith with others, the situation changes. Suddenly we discover that we haven't a clue about what our friends outside of church really believe. Small talk has obscured what lies in the hearts of our neighbors and work mates. Now we begin to see that if our witness is to be effective, if we are to make contact at all on any other than a superficial level, we will have to pay attention to all sorts of things we simply ignored before. We will need to learn about alternate spiritualities: New Age, Buddhism, Islam, Hinduism. We will need to listen closely to what people say when they are sharing their deepest concerns. We will find ourselves subscribing to different magazines, looking around, perhaps desperately, for books that can help us get a handle on the world we live in, talking to friends who are successful in bringing new people into the church. (For books that will help, see pp. 73-81.)

This will not be just a chore, something we do to be better apologists. It will begin to broaden our own understanding of the world. Then, when we add to this the study of Scripture with our culture in mind, we will find the content of our faith growing. Our faith will no longer be only privately engaging; it will be publicly relevant as well. We will become more and more able to communicate and defend the faith in ways that are relevant to the needs and issues of our day.

Apologetics, in short, is not just good for those we encounter; it is good for our own soul.

A STIMULUS TO A LIFE OF FULL COMMITMENT

One of the biggest reasons that people give for their rejection of the Christian faith is the hypocrisy of Christians themselves. "There are too many hypocrites in the church," we hear over and over. To which our only reply should be to say, "You're right," and then to live in such a way that it is never said nor even thought about us.

The practice of apologetics goes a long way to heighten a Christian's spiritual commitment, so as to produce what Schaeffer called *orthopraxy. Orthodoxy* is not enough. Not only do we need to know what the Christian faith is all about; we need to show that it is what we say it is by living it out. This itself is a powerful apologetic.

Christian faith is a faith that works. It works for individuals, and it works even more powerfully for communities, for churches and neighborhood Bible studies and campus Christian groups. A fully committed group of believers intentionally bent on living as a part of the kingdom of God on earth is in human form perhaps the very strongest of apologetics. Only Jesus himself is stronger. And even he is not alone, for the Trinity is always present with each of the Persons.

Apologetics is good not only for our soul but for our character and the character of our Christian community.

THE LIMITS OF APOLOGETICS

It may sound as if doing apologetics is the solution to all our problems, maybe even the sole key to spiritual growth, the only thing worth engaging in. Well, that would be false even on the face of it. The next chapter will look behind and beyond the face, for apologetics has lots of limits.

Ball State University and Tennessee Technical University

THE TIME WAS EARLY SPRING. The late evening was certainly not "spread out against the sky like a patient etherized upon a table," as it was in T. S. Eliot's "Love Song of J. Alfred Prufrock." Instead, thunderheads surrounded the small commuter plane that was flying me from O'Hare Airport in Chicago to Muncie, Indiana, to speak for InterVarsity Christian Fellowship at Ball State University. I could see the radar screen between the pilot and copilot and watched as we jigged and jagged between the dark masses to our right and left. Lightning flashed in the distance outside the windows.

When I arrived, I was met by a student who would be my host for the next day or so. Later I learned that of the small group of Christians who were sponsoring my time on campus, only one other wanted me to be there. The apologetic/evangelistic lecture I gave in a large hall in the student union did not go well. Perhaps fifteen people, some of whom appeared to be Christians from off campus, dotted the room. Most of the Christian groups did not attend. My voice disappeared into a void. Nothing happened. No questions. No comments. Nothing.

Years later the scene was the student union at Tennessee Technical University. As I walked down the hall with my student hosts, I could hear a hubbub in the auditorium and the whispers of students standing by a table behind which a large banner proclaimed "Why Should Anyone Believe Anything at All?" They nudged each other. "Look, here he comes," they said.

Excitement had been building for the previous few weeks as students prayed, invited their friends and, on the day of the lecture, surveyed the campus with the title question. Now the signal event was upon them. The room was filling with students. My host told me that earlier that day, one student had approached the survey table, looked at the sign and walked away. Then he had come back to take a survey form. Yet again he turned. "There's that question again. I've seen it all over campus. It makes my head hurt," he said and walked away for good. The question had torn the bandage from his aching heart. The evening went well.

The Limits of Apologetics

ALWAYS LURKING IN the back of my mind in the conversations I have with my friends is the thought: how can our conversation, in the long run, become an apologetic for some aspect of the Christian faith? Whether they are fellow believers in Christ, skeptics or those I just don't know well at all, I think: is there some way to make this encounter count for the truth of the gospel?

I think a lot about apologetics. Maybe I think about it too much. Maybe sometimes I should just live Christianly and let be what happens. Apologetics, after all, is not the be-all and end-all of the Christian life. It has too many limitations for that. Take these for example.

RATIONAL ARGUMENTS ARE OFTEN NOT INVOLVED IN COMING TO FAITH

Each year a number of apologetics books are published, and many more apologetic lectures are presented in universities and public forums. Many websites are devoted to apologetics, and Internet chatrooms harbor both givers and takers. Of course, some arguments are weak or just plain invalid. But many are not so obviously so. Yet nonbelievers seem seldom to change their mind on the basis of any given argument. When people do convert, they cite a host of factors that played a part. Sometimes "rational arguments" aren't even listed.

Notice, for example, the philosophers who contributed to *Philosophers Who Believe* and *God and the Philosophers*.[1] Thomas V. Morris speaks for many Christian philosophers when he says, "no amount of philosophical reasoning" gave him his religious picture of the world.[2] Philosopher C. Stephen Layman says that "few (if any) come to faith primarily because of evidence or arguments."[3]

> A proof . . . is something that will convince anyone who is intelligent enough to understand it. If so, very little of interest regarding major philosophical issues can be proved. This goes for issues in metaphysics, morality, political philosophy, and aesthetics. All or nearly of the major positions under these headings are highly controversial. There are brilliant people on either side of the interesting fences. So, if we demand proofs in philosophy, we will wind up as skeptics on all or nearly all of the important issues.[4]

In fact, in both books cited above only a few Christian philosophers indicate that they became believers because of an argument. Scholar and writer C. S. Lewis is usually cited as one who was converted through a process of reasoning. But, as *Surprised by Joy* implies throughout, there was a life context extending back to his childhood; his interest in fantasy and myth played a very great part. His nonrational (I don't say irrational) desire *(Sehnsucht)* for a final home, a place where all his dreams could be fulfilled, played a great role in his finding God, or as he would say, God's finding him. Likewise, Lewis long had an interest in mysticism and expressed this in both his fiction and nonfiction in what some might find as surprising ways.[5]

Again Morris speaks not only for himself but for me as well: "I am

a Christian because the deep resources of Christian theology reso-
nate with and make sense of both the contours of my experience and
the lineaments of my thought as I seek to gain a better theoretical
understanding of the world metaphysically, morally, aesthetically,
and epistemologically."[6]

Lest it appear that I am totally rejecting rational apologetics, let me
affirm strongly: there is a role for argument in the proclamation of the
gospel, especially for those arguments that answer objections. Nancy
Pearcey, for example, had abandoned her early Christian faith when
she ended up at L'Abri and encountered Francis A. Schaeffer and the
holistic apologetics of that intellectual and emotional healing community. Pearcey writes:

> While still at L'Abri I had once accosted a student, demanding
> that he explain why he had converted to Christianity. A pale,
> thin young man with a strong South African accent, he re-
> sponded simply, "They shot down all my arguments. . . . It's not
> always a big emotional experience, you know. . . . I just came to
> see that a better case could be made for Christianity than for
> any of the other ideas I came here with."[7]

She then says about her own conversion some time later: "As my
South African friend had put it, all my own ideas had been shot
down. The only step that remained was to acknowledge that I had
been persuaded—and then give my life to the Lord of Truth."[8]

Pearcey is recounting events in the early 1970s; ordinary rational arguments were much more effective in those "prepostmodern" days.
Still, with thoughtful people today, we may expect similar conversions.

REASONABLE EVIDENCE BUT NOT CERTITUDE
Certitude has long been a goal of humanity, and never more so than

in the past three hundred years. When René Descartes declared that he had found a way to get intellectual certitude, he changed the course of Western philosophy, shifting its primary concern from *being* (understanding what is there) to *knowing* (being certain that what we seem to know is true). The problem is that most philosophers think Descartes failed. No one, they believe, can have the sort of certitude he sought. Some in our postmodern world even challenge the notion of truth itself.

We must tread carefully here. Can we as Christians know that we have found the truth? How much confidence can we place in our apologetic arguments? Christian philosophers disagree on this point. Here are the polar positions.

First, following Thomas Aquinas, some philosophers place a great deal of emphasis on human reason. Yes, they say, we human beings are fallen; we can and do make mistakes. But the basic laws of thought remain solid, we can know what these are, and when we follow them, our arguments are valid. When our premises are true and our arguments are valid, then our conclusions are necessarily true.

Of course, we need true premises. But some of these are available through their own self-evidence (I exist; I have an idea of a perfect being; or I am being appeared to by the color red; or, more to the point at present, for example, I am being appeared to by something I believe is my computer or a book in which the present sentence exists). Some are the conclusions to valid arguments based on such self-evident premises. Aquinas would say, for example, that we cannot prove that Jesus is the Son of God by this method, but we can be assured that there is such a being as God (for example, a first cause, or a cosmic designer or a perfect being).

Other Christian philosophers and theologians are highly skeptical of human reason. They believe that the Fall has radically affected our ability to reason, so much so that only those who are redeemed can use their reason with confidence where spiritual matters are concerned, and even then reason is limited. Some would hold that even the laws of thought are not self-evidently true. Moreover, even if these laws are reliable, there is no way, they say, that one can be certain that what seems self-evident (one's own existence, for example) is in fact true. So there can be no reliably true premises on which to build a case, say, for the existence of God. Their alternative is to hold that every piece of knowledge we possess rests on beliefs that, strictly speaking, we may have evidence for but cannot prove beyond a shadow of a doubt. This does not mean that knowledge is not possible, only that it requires a fundamental commitment to notions like the orderliness of the universe, the general trustworthiness of our physical senses, the laws of thought and so forth. Belief and understanding are, in fact, linked. The classic expression of this is found in Augustine: "I believe in order to understand and I understand in order to believe." Note, however, that belief comes first. We cannot, for instance, prove beyond doubt (even to ourselves) that we are not dreaming, though we can give some rather convincing reasons.[9]

These two positions are mutually exclusive. Yet both are held by Christians. But here is the interesting point. It is not necessary for the practicing apologist to decide between them. Nor must he or she work out some reconciling midposition. Why? Because the argument is moot—outside the apologist's control. The practical *success* of any given apologetic argument lies solely with the audience.

Of course, the practicing apologist is interested in valid arguments based on premises that are true. Apologists love to succeed in establishing the faith of believers or in convincing nonbelievers to place their faith in Christ. Nonetheless, the skeptic is the one who decides whether an argument is persuasive or not. Each person holds his or her own premises; each person evaluates the plausibility of the apologist's argument. Each decides. So the question for the apologist is this: What do the skeptics—each of them individually—take as their fundamental beliefs? What is their worldview?

The writers of apologetic books can only make an intelligent guess as to what their readers will accept as rational. Christian apologists in dialogue with skeptics have a great advantage here. They can often discern just what the sticking point is.

Sometimes the sticking point is the historical reliability of the Gospels. So a case for their reliability will be in order. Sometimes the obstacle will be the very notion that any narrative of past events is reliable. Then the apologist can either examine this premise or shift to some apologetic that does not rely on the historical accuracy of Scripture. Sometimes the case can proceed by leaving aside the question of the accuracy of historical narratives and using these narratives simply as interesting stories that account for the belief of Christians and worth reading for their intrinsic interest or what they can tell us about Christians themselves. Scripture itself, through the presence of the Holy Spirit, has a way of getting beneath the typical objections made to its reliability. Jesus, as he emerges in the Gospels, is such a fascinating person that he looms before the reader as real apart from any rational defense of the Gospels' historical reliability.[10]

Philosopher Roy Clouser's comment and advice reflects my own take on the situation:

> Of course! Think it over. But I can tell you in advance that no amount of thinking it over will, all by itself, show you whether it's true. The experience I described, however, can. Read the Scriptures with as open a mind as you can muster. Listen to them as written from a commonsense point of view and as pos-

sible records of God's encounters with humans. Attend worship and Scripture study with a congregation of believers. Give yourself the best possible opportunity to have the same experience that I and millions of others have had. Only if that happens will you know why we believe in God.[11]

Sometimes the sticking point will be so basic that the apologist will have to start behind the tacit assumptions of the skeptic and undermine them. For example, if a skeptic says, "Truth is simply what one's society says it is" (one postmodern sort of premise), the "truth" of that premise will need to be challenged before any advance toward the demonstration of the truth of the gospel can proceed.[12]

In short, as apologists we can give reasonable evidence for the truths of the Christian faith, but we cannot offer knock-down proof, nor should we pretend to do so. A strictly intellectual apologetic can go only so far. Still, it is not only not irrational to go further, gathering an experiential grasp of the Christian faith, but it is utterly rational to do so.

EVIDENCE FOR THE TRUTH OF THE CHRISTIAN FAITH IS CUMULATIVE

It should be obvious, then, that a credible case for the Christian faith requires cumulative evidence. No one argument or even half-dozen arguments, as solid and convincing as they may be, will usually be sufficient to convince a serious skeptic. Of course, not every self-confessed skeptic is all that skeptical. Some think they are skeptical, but when presented with a basic outline of Christian faith they may quickly "see" the truth of Jesus Christ and place their faith in him. There is no predicting the course to faith any person will take.

Still, if a person has had little exposure to the Christian faith and manifests lots of reticence about making a life-changing commitment, there is little reason to think that just one telling argument—say for the existence of God or the resurrection of Jesus—will lead quickly to the conclusion that Jesus is Lord and Savior. On the one hand, the Christian gospel is quite simple; even a child can understand the rudiments. On the other hand, the simple gospel is so packed with rich concepts and counterintuitive notions (e.g., the Trinity, the deity of Christ, the resurrection) that an apologetic that addresses all the main concepts and answers all the most obvious objections (e.g., the problem of evil, how the Scriptures can be reliable, the unlikely story of the creation of Adam and Eve, the impossibility of miracles) must unite many interlocking arguments. A series of arguments, each of which gives independent (though not conclusive) reasons for differing elements of the Christian faith, can be like a rope of many strands. Each strand may give way when alone, but the combination of strands can be quite strong.

Apologists who learn to argue well for a few key doctrines and have answers to a few major objections may not find any skeptic who is impressed enough to pursue the issues further than the immediate dialogue. Becoming an effective apologist may take a very long time indeed.

INTELLECTUAL AGREEMENT IS NOT FAITH COMMITMENT

It should go without saying that we cannot induce a person to faith, piety, commitment or regeneration. Intellectual agreement is neither faith nor conversion. It may—in fact, it should—lead to faith. But often it doesn't. As the apostle James says, "Even the devils believe" that God is one, but their response is existential fear, not faith. They "shudder" (Jas 2:19).

The path to belief is mysterious. Sometimes facts and reasons stare us in the face. We can see them, even agree with them. Yet we turn away and don't act as if we knew them at all. At other times, we hear an argument and see the evidence, and before the case is fully made, something clicks. The penny drops. We find ourselves convinced and act accordingly. There are many reasons for this, but in any given instance we may not have a clue. Why did we fall in love—or out of love? Why did we think a particular politician was such a Godsend? We voted for him. When and why did we change our mind? Why don't we vote the same way a second time?

Lewis, describing a time when he was a theist but still not a Christian, makes this fascinating comment: "I was driven to Whipsnade one sunny morning. When we set out I did not believe that Jesus Christ is the Son of God, and when we reached the zoo I did. Yet I had not exactly spent the journey in thought. Nor in great emotion. . . . It was more like when a man, after long sleep, still lying motionless in bed, becomes aware that he is now awake."[13]

Roy Clouser recounts a similar experience: "A woman I know had been an outspoken atheist for years. She surprised me one day by speaking about God. When I asked how she came to believe, she said, 'Nothing really happened, I just woke up one morning and it all looked true. I have no explanation.'"[14]

Apologists as apologists are themselves not present in the process of a person's coming to belief. From the perspective of both the apologist and the believer, belief seems to be something that just happens. An apologist who has the joy of seeing a skeptic make the step to faith after reading one of his or her books or listening to a talk or participating in a conversation must not attribute the cause to the aptness of his or her apologetic. Rejoicing with the angels is quite enough.

APOLOGETICS AND THE HOLY SPIRIT

Sometimes after I have made an apologetic presentation, someone will say, "You have given all sorts of reasons why someone should believe. But I haven't heard you speak about the Holy Spirit. What is the role of the Holy Spirit in your apologetic?" My answer has been rather cryptic: "The Holy Spirit is nowhere and everywhere in my apologetic."

On the one hand, unless I am specifically talking about the doctrine of God, I do not mention the Holy Spirit directly. Nor do I imagine that once I have reached a certain point in my presentation I reach for a pitcher of the Holy Spirit and pour him into the bowl of the auditorium. There is no way I can release his power into the argument and the audience. The Holy Spirit cannot be manipulated. To try to do so is blasphemy. He plays no role that is under my control at all—ever!

But on the other hand, I desire the Holy Spirit to be everywhere in the apologetic. And he is. He is preparing those he has been calling to himself long before they hear anything I might say. He is in me as I prepare and make the presentation; he is in the presentation, and he is present to those who listen. He is the secret ingredient in every apologetic. He is the One who enlightens and brings people to faith; he is the One who lives in each believer to confirm that faith and foster spiritual growth from spiritual birth to eternity.[15]

Of course, prayer before, during and after one's presentation is always appropriate. But there is no particular "Holy Spirit way" for an apologist to prepare, no special "Holy Spirit technique" by which the presentation can be bettered. The Holy Spirit is nowhere (never to be used) and everywhere (always doing his thing).

THE HOLY SPIRIT AND PRAYER

Everything we have learned about prayer will be applicable to us as apologists. As in every other aspect of a Christian's life, prayer should always be at hand. So as apologists we should be praying every step of the way—for our study of Scripture and the world around us, for knowledge and sensitivity to the people we encounter, for those we meet and with whom we have significant conversations, for our community of faith to be an apologetic community, one living the faith we proclaim.

Such prayer bound a small group of InterVarsity students who, in the summer of 1991, spent several weeks in Sofia, Bulgaria. In a program of crosscultural study, they shared their faith with an equal number of Bulgarian students. By the time I arrived in Sofia in the fall, some half-dozen Bulgarians had become believers. One of them told me that the biggest reason the Bulgarian students were coming to Christ was the love that was shown in the community of Inter-Varsity Christians. The students not only studied together but also worshiped together. These Bulgarian students were now transmitting that love to their friends.

When I know I will be embarking on an apologetic mission, I ask my community to pray specifically for me and those I meet, for the situations to be conducive to good communication, for hearts and minds to listen and hear the gospel and respond in faith. That has been my practice since I began to lecture as a major part of my ministry.

I am not a very emotionally sensitive person. Just ask my friends! But there have been times, especially in Eastern Europe, when I have had a palpable sense of God's presence. Sometimes I would suddenly be taken aback by the ease with which I had just responded to what would normally have been a stressful experience.

In 1991 in Bucharest, on the second night of my lectures in the student union of the university, a Romanian guru touting the virtues of New Age nutrition refused to yield the auditorium when his time was up. The official managing the venue refused to ask the guru to yield the hall. Standing in small huddles at the back of the room, we Christians waited. I turned to the student near me and said, "I think we are in a spiritual battle tonight. Let's pray." Just as we began, the official, seeing that a great number of people were standing around waiting for my lecture, finally approached the guru and he stopped speaking. I thought the battle was over. But still he stayed on stage, taking questions and talking with some who came up to him. Calm as a gentle breeze on a spring evening, I went on stage and stood behind him, letting him see what I was doing. Embarrassed, I think, he finally left.

As the guru's audience filed out, they encountered a Christian booktable. Many of them bought copies of the Romanian edition of Lewis's *Mere Christianity*. Meanwhile some of the audience who had packed the hall stayed behind, joining those who came to my lecture. They heard my explanation and critique of Eastern mysticism and the New Age, permeated with a presentation of the gospel. When my audience filed out, even more Christian books went into the hands of people who had come primarily to listen to the guru.

Many times while traveling I have been asked to give a talk I had not prepared for or to speak to a person with whom I seemed to have very little in common. I would enter these situations with no trauma and only afterward realize that I had received a special gift directed not really to me but to those with whom I spoke.

As a sort of John Wesley on United Airlines (yes, I exaggerate grievously), I am not around for the local preparation for my university presentations. But as I began to travel, it soon became clear that four factors lay behind most of the successful events. Like the strands of a rope, each is intertwined with the others.

First, the lectures or discussions had student ownership. The sponsoring group—both its leaders and its ordinary members—

wanted the event to occur. When only InterVarsity staff or campus ministers or local pastors sponsored the events, on the other hand, they seldom drew enough attendance to be significant.

Second, the sponsoring group spent a lot of time in prayer—for their own attitudes, for their friends, for the glory of God, for the upcoming event.

Third, the students promoted the event with posters, brochures and sometimes questionnaires asking, for example, before my most popular talk: "Why should anyone believe anything at all?"

Fourth, the students specifically invited their friends. Their prayer had encouraged them to do so.

When these four factors came together, the event almost always drew two, three and sometimes four times the number of students in the sponsoring organization. When any one of these was missing, the results were seldom encouraging. But notice the role of prayer. Prayer works both ways—to transform the Christian sponsors and to alert the hearts and minds of skeptics and seekers. The Holy Spirit is not at our beck and call. But when we do call, he often comes.

HUMBLE APOLOGETICS

What, then, can we conclude about the values and limitations of apologetics? Let me return to the definition of apologetics given at the end of chapter one:

> Christian apologetics lays before the watching world such a winsome embodiment of the Christian faith that for any and all who are willing to observe there will be an intellectually and emotionally credible witness to its fundamental truth.

Apologetics has important values. It establishes the faith of believers, provides a defense of the faith to skeptics and seekers, heightens our understanding of our culture, and stimulates a life of full commitment to Jesus Christ as Lord and Savior. At the same time it has important limits. It cannot prove that Christianity is true beyond the shadow of a doubt, it requires a vast array of arguments and approaches to be close to complete, it cannot command a faith commitment, and while it relies on the action of the Holy Spirit, it cannot manipulate the Spirit to confirm the apologist's agenda.

What, then, is demanded is a *humble apologetic*—the apologist's reliance not on the cleverness or even the brilliance of argument but on the power of God to will and to do his good pleasure.[16]

Carnegie Mellon University, November 1995

OUTSIDE THE CAFETERIA where I was lecturing, two papers were being distributed, both written by atheists.

In "How Do You Know There Is a God?" Frank Zindler, a major spokesperson for an atheist society, presented a silly (not too strong a word) argument against claims that God exists. In "So . . . You Believe in God?" Barbara Smoker, president of the National Secular Society in Great Britain, bitterly railed against God, her major concern being that human suffering disproves the existence of a good and all-powerful deity. All this to knowledgeable Christians is standard stuff—not to be ignored, of course, but not to be given more respect than the arguments themselves deserve.

Inside, some seventy of us were discussing "reason enough" to believe anything including the Christian faith, comparing Nathanael (who leaped too quickly to identify Jesus as the "Son of God and King of Israel") and Thomas (who had to see Jesus' wounds before he would believe). Hot and heavy the dialogue proceeded, as it had the night before during my presentation of "Why Should Anyone Believe Anything at All?"

Finally a Christian asked, "How do you answer someone who is belligerent, argues poorly and seems utterly obtuse?"

"Observe," I responded, trying to suggest that I had been modeling the answer all evening. Then on went the dialogue with the skeptics, nihilists, seekers and quiet onlookers.

Often when a particularly nasty retort was voiced, the students turned on each other. Sometimes I just leaned back casually and let them have it out, coming in only at the end after they had destroyed each other's case. I simply pointed out the strength of the Christian position in light of the failure of the alternatives.

By the end of the evening, a self-confessed nihilist (one who holds that nothing can be shown to be true) had turned into an agnostic (one who doesn't know but thinks maybe one could know). Rick the joker, who reduced everything to "cool" or "not cool," had lost the respect of the other students just by being allowed to speak long enough to hang himself. A less vocal nihilist who spoke volumes by his nonverbal behavior left as bitter as he came.

The Christian students were thrilled to see how well the Christian faith stood the tests for truth and remained solid despite the volume, tone and weight of criticism. One woman who had come to have her faith strengthened found her faith challenged but more muscular by the end. During the two evenings, non-Christians verbally wrestled with each other, their Christian friends and me. Perhaps a dozen indicated an interest in further study of the Gospels.

4

The Contexts of Apologetics

APOLOGETIC ARGUMENTS take place in a variety of contexts. One of the reasons they often do not work—that is, do not persuade—is that they are cast in ways that are inappropriate to the situation. There's a great difference between an apologist's presentation of a case for the Christian faith to a large audience and that same apologist's chat with a small group around a table at Starbucks or one-to-one dialogue with a friend. The tone and temper of the atmosphere, its openness or hostility, its formality or informality, its time constraint or lack thereof are all significant.

To survey the contexts, let's begin with the more formal and more hostile situations, drawing on my experiences both as an apologist and as a person in the audience.

FORMAL LECTURES TO PRIMARILY NONBELIEVING AUDIENCES

Picture this situation. I have been invited to present a case for the Christian faith to a group of university students at a small, elite private college. The organization sponsoring the event is the local chapter of InterVarsity Christian Fellowship. There are about sixty students in the room, only about twenty of whom are known to be

Christians. Much prayer has gone into the students' preparation for this event. No one, especially me, believes that the event is certain to be successful—in this case, meaning that some nonbelievers will be attracted enough by what transpires to dig further into the Christian faith and eventually to commit their lives to Christ. We, the students and I, are thinking of this event as evangelistic, but not in the sense that we expect conversions during or immediately afterward. The lecture is rather preevangelistic—preparing the ground and sowing some seed. The main practical goal is to get students to participate in student-led Bible studies in which they will be able to assess for themselves the character of Jesus Christ.

What must I realize before I begin? A host of things! Here are four. First, I must realize that I can take nothing for granted with this group. In fact, it is likely that some have come out of curiosity, some because they have been invited by a friend and are being polite, others because they want to show off their ability to "stump the chump" who would deign to bring a backwater faith to an avant-garde college. But there may also be others who are secretly seeking answers to troubling spiritual questions. Many—perhaps most, and this is especially sad to say—will have a distorted idea about what the central features of traditional Christianity actually are. They will have even less understanding of Jesus, the person whom I will be intent on their eventually coming to know and love. Even those who are believers may be unaware of some central features of the faith. So my explanations will have to be clear without being simplistic. I must respect their intellect while not assuming that they know much about what I will be presenting.

Second, I must realize that I will be the focus of attention, and I will have to win the right to be heard. That is, I need to establish credibility. College students who are not already aware of who you are and what you represent can be a tough audience. They have some excellent teachers, and I will be measured at least in part by reference to them. So I will need to be accurate. I must not just pretend that I know what I am talking about but actually do so.

In one such lecture at Grinnell, an elite private school, early in my years of lecturing, I made two serious errors in the first of three presentations that were to extend over three days. My first talk was intended to show that Christianity's understanding of reality is superior to that of the "beat" take on reality that was still attracting students in the 1970s. I lost my audience, first, by presenting Gerard Manley Hopkins's "God's Grandeur" almost as if it were a biblical text. Reflecting back, I realized that I had not just explicated the poem but *preached* it. The lounge of the student union was full when I started, but within ten minutes, students began leaving. Half had left in the first thirty minutes. They did not stay to hear me make my second mistake. I tried to use a poem by Lawrence Ferlinghetti to illustrate the thinking of a poet who did not understand the crucifixion. But I had misread it! I had missed the ironic tone and utterly distorted its meaning. Worse, some of the students recognized my mistake.

Some of these were the Christian students who were sponsoring the talks. There was no hiding the failure by suggesting to them that the audience rejected the truth because they were hostile or ignorant or willfully perverse. They knew I had lost the audience all on my own. Worse, I had to remain on campus two more days. They had to bear the embarrassment of being my host. I have made mistakes since, but so far as I know I never made these two again.

What should I have done? Certainly the chief failure was rhetorical. I should have started first with the view I wished to counter. I could have done this easily by choosing a powerful poetic expression of the beat view, emphasizing its high aesthetic quality, unpacking its subtler elements, thus illustrating the quality of my grasp of the poem and its meaning. In other words, I could have won the right to continue toward the aim of my lecture: to show the equally high, or higher, aesthetic quality of the poem and the superior grasp of reality displayed by Hopkins. Would the audience have walked out anyway? It's hard to tell, but there would have been far less rational reason for them to do so. In any case, since then such a mass exodus has never recurred.

Third, I must respect the students to whom I speak. That means that if I tell a joke or use humor in any way—and I always try to do so—I should never make them the butt of the story. Much better that I should do that to myself. For example, I have often referred in my lectures to Jesus' calling the disciples. The Gospel of John tells how Jesus found Philip, who then found Nathanael, who identified Jesus of Nazareth as the Messiah. Nathanael then replies (in my version), "Can any good thing come out of Chicago?" This usually gets a laugh. Sometimes at, say, the University of Michigan, I would say, "Can any good thing come from Ohio State?" But never, never ever, as one who graduated from the University of Nebraska and now lives in Chicago, would I say, "Can any good thing come from the University of Michigan?"

Fourth, I must maintain credibility while projecting genuine humility. This doesn't mean saying to an audience, "I really don't know what I am talking about," but rather holding my self-confidence lightly, not taking my expertise too seriously. One way to show this is by being open to and respecting the integrity of others who hold contrary opinions.

I once heard a lecturer on a cruise ship headed south along the coast of Chile to round Cape Horn and eventually arrive in Rio de Janeiro. He had or pretended to have (I'm not sure which) credentials that included having been a diplomat with personal knowledge of all sorts of people involved in the running of South America and the world. He projected such certainty that when he said something I knew not to be true, I nudged a woman next to me and said, "That's not true." Her response was "Neither was that," referring to a different remark. Speakers can make errors—even basic ones—and not lose their audience only if they hold their obvious intelligence and grasp of the subject project with a large measure of humility. I did not attend his next lecture.

THE QUESTION-AND-ANSWER PERIOD

I love to get questions after my presentations.[1] Questions allow me to clarify my presentation and often expand on it. They also allow me to respond directly to issues that the audience has found interesting. Sometimes in an academic situation they allow me to make my presentation more personal, both for me and for the audience. That privilege comes with such questions as "How can I know that I am actually getting to the truth?" or "I want to believe, but I just can't yet do so. What can I do?" or "How did you become a believer?" or "Surely there are more options than 'liar, lunatic or Lord,' aren't there? What about this? 'Jesus was just a little wrong about himself. His moral teaching is what's important.'"

But for me there are at least three reasons that these questions sometimes do not come. My friend (and boss) James Nyquist pointed out one of these. "Jim," he said, "in your talks you tie up all the loose ends. You need to leave some things unsaid." He was right. I still need to leave my lectures somewhat open-ended and thus intriguing. I've tried to take Jim's advice but have had only modest success.

The second reason questions sometimes do not come is that I have exhausted too much of the available time. Even if I raised lots of unresolved issues, I haven't left enough time for questions.

Third, sometimes the culture gets in the way. In Eastern Europe in the 1990s after the Berlin Wall came down, for example, the audience was starved for anything fresh and noncommunistic. They tended to have great staying power, willing to sit on hard benches for two or three hours. But they were not used to asking questions of their professors. The professor was the *authority*. His or her word, even if obviously wrong or foolish, was law. To counter this, my sponsors (often the International Fellowship of International Students [IFES]) would pass out sheets of paper for questions; after the lecture, these would be passed to the front, where I could select and answer them. Always the point was to get as much personal interaction with the audience as possible.

When questions do come, they are often hard to understand in the way the questioner has understood them. Whenever I sense that this is the case, I ask for clarification, sometimes for meaning, sometimes for context. It is more often the latter that is hard to understand. I have a ready answer for a number of standard questions, but my ready answers may be totally off the point. "How can a good God make a world that has so much evil in it?" may not be answered by any version of the "freewill defense." It may really have better been framed as "Why is my six-year-old brother dying of cancer?"

It is often a good idea to answer a question with a question, not just to give you time to frame an answer but to make sure your answer gets to the issue.[2] An apologist's good question often reveals that the questioner is trying to "stump the chump" at the podium, not searching for truth. Take this question: "What is the most difficult question you have ever been asked?"

If I took this question at face value, I could mention questions that have revealed various aspects of my ignorance. Here's one I actually received in an university classroom in Zagreb, Croatia: "I have been persuaded by Max Scheler on the topic you address, but his view seems different from yours. How do you view Scheler's take on this subject?" I responded by saying I was unfamiliar with Scheler's views and asked for clarification. When I got it, I made a few probably not very astute comments and went on to the next question.[3] I have no idea if I lost credibility at that point. It might have been just as well to have said I was unable to answer the question. To have given an obscure response in order to obfuscate and conceal my ignorance would surely have been ill advised. Never pretend. Pretense is almost always detected, and credibility is utterly lost.

Actually, perhaps the most troubling questions I have had to answer are various versions of questions about evil. I have worked out responses to these questions, of course. And I have often used them to focus on the cross, where Jesus shows how much God participates in human suffering. The good news of the gospel thus gets a chance to be illustrated in reference to an issue that in the final analysis I have to say remains a mystery to me, as it does even to many of those who have addressed it thoughtfully.[4]

Still, as I recall, when I was asked, "What is the most difficult question you have ever been asked?" I decided that the question might not be serious. It might even be nasty, intended to make me reveal my ignorance. Despite the value of being humble as well as being thought humble, I didn't think I needed to be humiliated.

So I said, "The question you have just asked."

The audience laughed and we went on to the next question.

FORMAL LECTURES TO PRIMARILY CHRISTIAN AUDIENCES

As we saw above, Christians can benefit greatly from apologetics. So another context of apologetics is formal lectures to Christians. On the one hand, this audience appears to be much "easier." But it too has its hazards and its demands.

Let us say that I am addressing a group of Christians on the intellectual character of the university world in order to help them understand what they are currently experiencing. As I write this, I have just addressed a university Sunday school class in the Seattle area. Most of the students are attending secular institutions, and their regular teacher asked me to give a lecture I call "The University in Two Minds: Modern and Postmodern." I have spoken on this topic many times in the previous fifteen years or so. What must I keep in mind as I prepare and deliver the current talk?

First, I must understand the audience. Here I can take some things for granted. Most of the students will be believers. I will not need to argue for the Christian faith. I only need to show how it is relevant to the situation they face on campus, especially in their classrooms and among their college friends. From experience I know that most of the students will have heard the word *postmodern* but that only a few in the humanities and the social sciences will be able to define it. The same students who have never heard the word may have unwittingly absorbed aspects of postmodernism that have distorted their Christian faith without their knowing it. Those Christians who are conscious of postmodernism may actually be persuaded that it offers a good understanding of reality. Those in the sciences, even when they hear it defined and get a basic grasp of the concept, will usually be baffled by it. They will wonder how anyone could think such a thing. The fact is: any general audience in the educated world will be made up of all these sorts of people. I will need to keep that in mind.

Second, I will need to organize and present the content of the lecture in light of this diverse audience, trying to take those with a basic understanding of modernity and postmodernity more deeply into the subject, especially in regard to how both compare and contrast with a Christian worldview. But the material must be made intelligible to those with very little background in either philosophy or sociology—the main academic disciplines that address the concepts. My primary goal will be to enable all the students to understand the intellectual ethos of their college culture and through this to ease the tension many students feel as their faith is marginalized and challenged by this culture. Beyond this, too, I wish to help them see how their Christian faith gives them a better understanding of, and ability to cope with, reality than either modernity or postmodernity does.

Each Christian audience will, of course, be different. There are multigenerational church groups, students at Christian colleges, Christian students at secular universities and even Saturday morning men's groups. Every presentation needs to be adapted.

INFORMAL PRESENTATIONS TO SMALL GROUPS

In small groups informality should be the order of the day. Once at the University of Missouri I heard the stentorian voice of a history professor lecturing to what from the doorway appeared to be an empty room. Curious, I stuck my head in the door, where I saw the professor with his back to me lecturing full bore to one student.

A casual attitude and tone are a great advantage in reaching people's hearts and minds. This does not, however, mean abandoning a structured presentation. It does mean that, if a small group is the context of my apologetic presentation, I should be prepared to pause for questions at key points, be willing to be interrupted by questions and comments, and be gracious in responding. Respect for participants is, of course, crucial.

One of the most fascinating small groups I've ever been involved in gathered unwittingly in a train compartment in Italy. Three university professors were en route from Rome to Cosenza. With my host, IFES staff member Tom Balma, and my translator, Deborah

Favareto, I shared a compartment with them for six hours. After several hours, the ice broke, and they wondered what such an unlikely trio was doing on the train. When they found out the title of my lecture, "Why Should Anyone Believe Anything at All?" the conversation took off.

"I don't think there are any good reasons," the ethnomusicologist said. "People just believe what they were raised to believe. And that's okay. Whatever they believe is fine."

"But contradictory beliefs can't both be true," I countered, and that sparked the dialogue.

The physicist turned out to be a deist with a few theistic leanings. Given the complex unity of the physical world, he couldn't believe the universe is just an accident. There must be some kind of God. But given the suffering in the world, he didn't know quite what to make of this God. Still, there was Dante, especially the line "Faith is the substance of things hoped for and the evidence of things not seen," which he quoted, not realizing that Dante got this from the Letter to the Hebrews. He rested in hope.

"I can't believe anything religious in particular," the professor of stage design said. "I don't think anything can be shown to be true."

We had several hours to bat around these ideas. I had ample opportunity to explain in more detail that Dante had much more than a one-line credo. I was able to casually recount the basic gospel story and to say why I thought it was true.

By the end, the physicist was arguing my case against the ethnomusicologist. "Two contradictory propositions can't both be true," he expostulated.

So go apologetic small groups. In college we used to call them "bull sessions." Sometimes they become events unwitting participants look back on as prompting them to faith in Christ.

PRIVATE CONVERSATIONS

Apologetic arguments in private conversations should always be, as much as possible, low key and calm. There is no place for bluster, no place for aggressive confrontation and no place for anger. There is every place for asking probing questions and listening carefully before presenting one's views. Most of Jesus' recorded conversations were held in public. But the one in John 4 as Jesus speaks with the woman at the well is a model of give-and-take, probing questions, insightful answers and stellar focus on matters that are central to Christian faith.

I have only very dim memories of most of the countless dialogues I have had with nonbelievers over the past forty years. But I do recall one student, perhaps because he was in a wheelchair and was introduced to me by InterVarsity staff member Ken Vander Wall at lunchtime in a cafeteria at William Paterson State College in New Jersey. In the past, he had asked Ken a number of questions. Now he asked me. I have no memory of their content—perhaps the problem of evil, perhaps something of the reasons for trusting the Gospel accounts, perhaps something unique and personal. But I do know that the conversation went well, because Ken told me a few weeks later that this student traced his conversion at least in part to our conversation.

Other conversations have seemingly gone less well and have involved some necessary confrontation. A young student at Ulster University in Jordanstown, Northern Ireland, approached me after I had given an apologetic lecture. The dialogue went something like this.

"Now, if I understand you, you just said that you can't prove that God exists."

"Yes, I said that."

"Okay. So that means that I can believe anything I want. Right?"

"No," I said. "You should believe whatever is true, not just whatever you want. God either exists or he doesn't exist. If he does exist, then you are responsible to him. There is plenty of evidence that God in fact does exist. I outlined that in my lecture. To believe that he exists and that you are responsible to him is the most rational response. To obey God is the most rational thing you can do."

"Yes, but you can't prove it. Right?"

"Right. I can't demonstrate with full philosophical certainty that God exists."

"Right. So I can believe anything I want," he said again.

"Sure. You can believe anything you want, but if you are wrong you will be held responsible. And God is a pretty stern judge." I tried to help him see that his religious beliefs involved high stakes.

"Yes, but you can't prove that God exists."

The conversation was a loop. Around and around we went. Finally, as he walked away, I yelled after him, "You're not off the hook."

During this time a young woman had been listening to this exercise in argumentative futility. When the young man left, she said, eyes welling up with tears, "You know, if God doesn't exist, life is really futile. But I just can't believe he does." What an odd pleasure to hear this comment. Here was an honest seeker whom it was possible to help. I do not remember what I said to her, probably something about reading Scripture and asking God, if he exists, to reveal himself to her. Or perhaps, as I often do, I gave her the advice Rebecca Manley Pippert has given to others: Read the Scriptures, begin to live as they command, and pray to God—or to the four walls—that if he exists he will reveal himself in some way.[5]

This woman's reaction illustrates a principle I think it is important for an apologist to realize. Apologetic arguments are often more effective when they are overheard than when they are directed at a specific person. This is especially true when the one you are speaking to is surrounded by friends. No one wants to lose an argument, no one wants to be embarrassed by having to change his or her mind in public—and few do or, if they do, let on that they do. But those who overhear a conversation do not lose face; they can be persuaded and are much more likely to agree with a sound argument than is either person in the dialogue.[6]

This means that while I am conversing with a person in the question-and-answer part of a lecture, I am concerned to make a good case regardless of whether it is accepted by the one asking the question or raising an objection. Those who overhear the dialogue may come to agree with me.

Conversational apologetics often emerges as unexpected joyful encounters turn to matters of common spiritual interest. At Trenton State University, now called the College of New Jersey, I met Mike in a campus coffee shop. Mike was a music teacher, a friend of Jim McCullough, my InterVarsity student host. Our conversation began with sharing our mutual interest in open nature—the Colorado Rockies. Then it quickly moved to a mutual interest in spiritual matters, those Mike and Jim had been discussing for some time as their faculty-student friendship had developed through Jim's four years as a music major. Soon deep, penetrating issues surfaced. Is Jesus really the only way to God? Can't I have a bit of Eastern metaphysics on the side? What about sin? Mike would have liked to have the pleasant things of Christian faith without the unpleasant.

Did Mike move toward faith? I don't know. But I do know I prayed for him and had my friends do so as well. Apologists often must enter these conversations in faith that God has an end in mind and then leave the ongoing witness to others and the results to the Holy Spirit, taking joy in the privilege of witnessing to the truth of God in Christ reconciling the world to himself.

LONG-TERM RELATIONSHIPS

Certainly the best context for apologetics is a long-term friendship. I have a few friends in various stages of commitment to Christ. Some are clearly nonbelievers and seem only tentatively open to apologetics for the Christian faith. Others are some way further along the path and may well be Christians who need to see more deeply into the nature of genuine Christian belief and behavior. Still others are Christians with whom I share some deep spiritual truths. It is in such a context that arguments for various aspects of a Christian worldview can be most fully pursued with the most likelihood of comprehension.

Mutual respect, of course, dominates this context. We appreciate and have the best in mind for each other. We comfort each other in sorrow, help each other in sickness and enjoy each other's company. In this situation I find myself not so much projecting my own views and attempting to persuade by good reason and good rhetoric as simply being one beggar trying to help another beggar to find bread. (This is E. Stanley Jones's definition of evangelism.)

There is, of course, a danger inherent in this context. I can so privilege our relationship that I fear the effect of challenging my friend's false or inadequate views. As a result, I can fail to present the truth that will bring us both to a fuller knowledge of God. But if I keep in mind that the bread we seek together is the bread of life in Jesus Christ, I will be much less inclined to waver in my witness.

ALWAYS BE PREPARED

Finally, there is the obvious context of chance encounters. People who travel a lot have many opportunities to engage in significant apologetic conversations. When you travel, what should you be thinking?

For one thing, you may develop a set way to insert Jesus or your faith into the dialogue. Some evangelism teachers suggest asking the question "Are you interested in spiritual things?" I have always felt that this is hokey. If anyone said that to me, my guard would go up and my suspicion would be triggered. *Here is a religious nut,* I would think. Better for me has been to be sensitive to interests that people demonstrate on their own initiative. Still, I do not want to discourage such a set approach for those who don't find it awkward or aggressive.

I'd rather have a more natural approach stemming from the context itself. For example, on a flight from Europe to Chicago, a young woman was intently reading a book that I could see from the title was New Age in perspective. We had seven hours to spend together, so I relaxed and thought about how I could stimulate a spiritual dialogue. Finally, I simply asked her what her book was about. She told me it was all about how she could enhance her self-image by certain practices and beliefs. Suddenly, she blurted out, "You know, I've just spent three weeks in England with my friend, and she was so selfish. She wanted to make all the decisions about what we did and where we went. I had a miserable time." It was easy then for me to suggest that she return to her Christian roots for spiritual insight and guidance.

She didn't need a critique of the book she was reading. She just needed to recognize what following its teachings would mean. All this stemmed from a simple question about what she was reading.

On a much shorter flight, the businessman next to me was taciturn until he ordered a drink. After this he opened up by asking, "Have you ever read *The Late Great Planet Earth?*" At the time it was a best-selling, rather scary book on Christian eschatology. Our dialogue was off and running. The key is to pay attention to the interests of others and adapt your own presentations to that.

I must confess, though, that though I have accumulated thousands of frequent flyer miles, I have not been very successful in generating significant spiritual conversations. Do I not have this aspect of the "gift of evangelism"? Or am I remiss in not learning because I have been reticent in initiating specifically spiritual topics?

Better here for me to leave those questions open than to make any recommendations from my own experience on how readers should act. The principle is clear, however: "Always be ready to make your defense to anyone who demands from you an accounting for the hope that is in you" (1 Pet 3:15).

Southern Illinois University, February 1990

AT SOUTHERN ILLINOIS UNIVERSITY, an auditorium filled to overflowing with some four hundred people who came to hear a dialogue between Dr. Donald Paige and me. Paige, a professor of math education who once told a class that unless they were into higher consciousness they were an impediment to education, maintained a full-fledged New Age position.

Paige identified the New Age with five points: (1) a strong belief in God as a creative force and human beings as sparks of the divine, as many paths lead to God; (2) inspired information—the Qur'an, the Bible, the Book of Mormon and the Upanishads are all inspired, and so are many channeled materials, like those from Ra and the Course in Miracles; (3) reincarnation—Paige predicted that by the year 2000 most Christians would believe in reincarnation; (4) out-of-body travel; (5) and crystals—though Paige himself rejects these as having any psychic power.

I countered with a presentation of Christian spirituality as the relationship between a holy God and his redeemed people. Then came lots of dialogue between us and many questions from the audience. When asked about how so many contradictory writings could be inspired, Paige responded that they all teach love and harmony among people and respectful treatment of the earth. Each religious tradition, he said, is like a tube down which one looks toward a common ultimate reality. One need only be faithful to the vision of one's own tradition. To say this, of course, is to abandon rationality as a useful category for discrimination. He found no problems with doing so.

So who came to the dialogue? Some 320 cards were distributed. According to the 208 cards turned in, there were 135 Christians, 41 New Agers, 26 who were neither—and 6 who said they were both. Some 61 people wanted more information either on Christianity or the New Age.

5

The Arguments of Apologetics

THE ARGUMENTS OF APOLOGETICS—what a vast subject! This is just a primer. To cover this topic adequately would, quite frankly, take a very large volume indeed. What I can do is list some of the major types of arguments and recommend sources where they are elaborated enough to become useful for apologists who are just getting started.

Here are the main arguments that set forth a positive case for the truth of the Christian faith. I will begin with the positive arguments, then list the ways to answer objections to Christian claims.

THE POSITIVE CASE FOR CHRISTIAN FAITH

The case from Jesus. I am convinced that the strongest case for the Christian faith is Jesus himself. This may not appear to be an argument, but it is. What, after all, are we arguing for? Is it not that Jesus is the Christ, the Son of the living God, Savior and Lord of the universe? If so, then meeting Jesus will be all that is required.

And where do we meet Jesus? In some ways, he is present in everything we see, touch, feel and smell, for Jesus is present in the world as both its creator and its sustainer. He "sustains all things by his powerful word" (Heb 1:3). But without the redeemed mind at work, his presence in the world is not likely to be noticed. Not to worry. He made himself known visibly when he lived on Earth, his disciples have testified to who he is, and the Gospels that they wrote, inspired as they are by the Holy Spirit, pour forth a powerful witness to both his earthly and his transcendent reality. Jesus comes to us through the pages of the Gospels.

So what is our argument? Come and meet him. Come and see. See him come alive before you as you read the Gospels.

It's a simple argument. Do you want to know my wife? I can tell you about her. But if you really want to know her, you must meet her. And when you do, you will tend to forget everything I had said about her. So it is with Jesus.

Of course, it is not easy to get people on their own to read Matthew, Mark, Luke and John. Sometimes people will come to small group Bible studies or attend a lecture on Jesus or join you at church. The chief argument, however, is none of these. It is Jesus himself.

The apologist, then must strive to know Jesus intimately. That means intensive reading of the Gospels and solid books about Jesus. There are many. Here are a few of the most introductory and the best:

Sire, James W. *Why Should Anyone Believe Anything at All?* Downers Grove, Ill.: InterVarsity Press, 1994.

Stott, John R. W. *Basic Christianity.* 2nd ed. Downers Grove, Ill.: InterVarsity Press, 1970.

Wright, N. T. *Who Is Jesus?* Grand Rapids, Mich.: Eerdmans, 1992.

Yancey, Philip. *The Jesus I Never Knew.* Grand Rapids, Mich.: Zondervan, 1995.

The historical reliability of the Gospels. The argument from Jesus requires a minimal acceptance of the Gospels as a reliable record of what Jesus said and did. It does not require a seeker to believe in the inerrancy or infallibility of the Scriptures, only to give some credence to its honest recording of events that really happened. Numerous books can help. In my estimation, here are the best:

Barnett, Paul. *Is the New Testament Reliable?* Downers Grove, Ill.: InterVarsity Press, 1986.

Blomberg, Craig. *The Historical Reliability of the Gospels.* Downers Grove, Ill.: InterVarsity Press, 1987.

Dunn, James D. G. *The Evidence for Jesus.* Philadelphia: Westminster Press, 1986.

France, R. T. *The Evidence for Jesus.* Downers Grove, Ill.: InterVarsity Press, 1986.

Wright, N. T. *The Contemporary Quest for Jesus.* Minneapolis: Fortress, 2002.

The internal coherence of the Christian worldview. Everyone has a basic take on life—a more or less consistent way of understanding the world in which we live. It is also more or less conscious, but conscious or not, it forms the backdrop of all our thinking. For Christians, the most foundational aspect of our worldview is our understanding of God as personal, good, loving, triune, all powerful, totally intelligent and everywhere present. This fundamental commitment, when well understood, can be seen to account for all of our experience, all of our knowledge. In fact it accounts for it better than any other alternative, such as naturalism (the material world is all there is) or pantheism (God and the world are the same) or New Age thought (somehow you yourself are divine). The Christian worldview makes more sense of even the toughest issues (the problem of suffering, for example) than any of the alternatives. In my book mentioned below, I have tried not only to set forth a case for the Christian faith but to argue for its superiority to seven alternatives (deism, naturalism, nihilism, existentialism, Eastern pantheism, the New Age and postmodernism).

The argument from the superiority of the Christian worldview will require considerable study, but as you engage in such study, you will come to understand your own commitment to Christ in much greater depth. You will also gain confidence in setting forth your own case for the Christian faith.

Pearcey, Nancy. *Total Truth: Liberating Christianity from Its Cultural Captivity.* Wheaton, Ill.: Crossway, 2004.

Sire, James W. *The Universe Next Door.* 4th ed. Downers Grove, Ill.: InterVarsity Press, 2004.

Arguments for individual aspects of the Christian faith. There are a host of arguments for key aspects of the Christian faith: the existence of God, the deity of Christ, the resurrection of Jesus, the exclusivity of the Christian faith, the rationality of belief in miracles, the immateriality of the soul, and the fact of a life after death. None of these arguments by itself is adequate as a final *proof* for Christian faith, but they show that it is not irrational to hold these beliefs with full intellectual confidence, not just subjective certainty.

Of the tens, maybe hundreds of books, dealing with these issues, the following are head and shoulders above most of the rest:

Kreeft, Peter, and Ronald K. Tacelli. *Handbook of Christian Apologetics: Hundreds of Answers to Crucial Questions.* Downers Grove, Ill.: InterVarsity Press, 1994.

Moreland, J. P. *Scaling the Secular City: A Defense of Christianity.* Grand Rapids, Mich.: Baker, 1987.

Personal experience of God. I rather imagine that the first reason many of us Christians will give for the certainty of our faith is our personal experience of God in Christ. Our argument goes like this: Once I was lost—confused, anguished by guilt, disgusted with myself, troubled about my worth, my identity. Then I found Jesus—or Jesus found me—and everything changed. I am a new person with a new spring in my step. Jesus has saved me and set me free to be who he meant for me to be. I invite you, I invite everyone, to place your faith in Jesus.

This can make a strong emotional appeal and is often an effective apologetic, even though strictly speaking it is weak philosophically. If taken as an argument, it commits the fallacy of hasty generalization, and it ignores the testimony of those who have found satisfaction in non-Christian religions or in no religious faith at all. But it still should be an important part of any Christian's case for his or her faith. For if Christianity is true, these experiences should occur. They do testify to the truth of the Christian faith.

There are countless biographies and autobiographies that supply marvelous accounts of the richness of life in Christ. Here are a few:

Colson, Charles. *The Good Life: Seeking Purpose, Meaning and Truth in Your Life*. Wheaton, Ill.: Tyndale House, 2005.

Downing, David. *The Most Reluctant Convert: C. S. Lewis's Journey to Faith*. Downers Grove, Ill.: InterVarsity Press, 2002.

Goricheva, Tatiana. *Talking About God Is Dangerous*. Trans. John Bowden. New York: Crossroad, 1987.

Lewis, C. S. *Surprised by Joy: The Shape of My Early Life*. London: Geoffrey Bles, 1955.

Mumma, Howard. *Albert Camus and the Minister*. Brewster, Mass.: Paraclete, 2000.

Stott, John R. W. *Why I Am a Christian*. Downers Grove, Ill.: InterVarsity Press, 2004.

ANSWERS TO OBJECTIONS TO CHRISTIAN FAITH

The problem of evil. There is no question in my mind that the problem of evil and suffering is the toughest challenge to Christian faith. Why would a God who is good create a world in which there is so much evil and suffering? Is he not all powerful? Or is he not really good after all?

It has taken a long time for me to come to terms with this problem in such a way that I can make responses to it when challenged by a skeptic. If you wish to see what I have written, you will find it in *Why Should Anyone Believe Anything at All?*[1] For a much more detailed treatment (and indeed an apologist should go deeper), I most highly recommend these books:

Blocher, Henri. *Evil and the Cross.* Translated by David G. Preston. Downers Grove, Ill.: InterVarsity Press, 1994.

Kreeft, Peter. *Making Sense Out of Suffering.* Ann Arbor, Mich.: Servant, 1986.

Wenham, John. *The Enigma of Evil: Can We Believe in the Goodness of God?* Grand Rapids, Mich.: Zondervan, 1985.

Evolution as an explanation for everything. The answer to the challenge of evolution is both more and less complex than Christians commonly think. On the one hand, a Christian does not need to be concerned by the fact that changes in the cosmos or the biosphere have taken place over vast reaches of time. God could have used processes of gradual change as his method of bringing about the current highly complex and orderly cosmos, human beings included.

On the other hand, the notion that such change can be explained solely by the forces of nature without invoking any notion of intelligence or design means that the beauty and apparent design of the universe do not testify to the existence of God. It would mean, contrary to the ancient psalmist, that the heavens do not proclaim the glory of God (Ps 19). And contrary to the apostle Paul, it would mean that what we see in the universe does not point to God's "eternal power and divine nature" (Rom 1:20). Rather the theory of evolution removes any good reason for believing that God exists at all. As biologist Richard Dawkins has said, "Darwin made it possible to be an intellectually fulfilled atheist."[2]

Christians need to know that Dawkins is wrong about the explanatory power of the theory of evolution. They need to know that the biblical notion of God as Creator explains what scientists can observe in nature far better than any combination of chance and necessity. Dawkins is simply wrong when he says, "It is absolutely safe to say that if you meet somebody who claims not to believe in evolution, that person is ignorant, stupid, or insane (or wicked, but I'd rather not consider that)."[3]

The stack of Christian responses to evolutionary theory is just about a mile high. Sorting out the best for those beginning to understand the challenge is difficult. Here is my attempt. Start with those by Blocher and Johnson.

Blocher, Henri. *In the Beginning: The Opening Chapters of Genesis.* Downers Grove, Ill.: InterVarsity Press, 1984.

Carlson, Richard F., ed. *Science and Christianity: Four Views.* Downers Grove, Ill.: InterVarsity Press, 2000.

Dembski, William. *The Design Revolution: Answering the Toughest Questions About Intelligent Design.* Downers Grove, Ill.: InterVarsity Press, 2004.

Johnson, Phillip E. *Darwin on Trial.* 2nd ed. Downers Grove, Ill.: InterVarsity Press, 1993.

Ratzsch, Del. *Science and Its Limits: The Natural Sciences in Christian Perspective.* 2nd ed. Downers Grove, Ill.: InterVarsity Press, 2000.

Relativism and the exclusivity of truth. The chief current, "postmodern," objection to Christianity is that no religion, including Christianity, tells it like it really is. Every claim to truth is a human construction. Any construction, any religion or nonreligion, that gets you what you want can be true for you but need not be true for anyone else. This challenge undercuts every traditional claim to truth—both atheism and theism. To most Christians this seems like a strange notion indeed. But it is rife in the university world, especially in the humanities and the social sciences. An apologist needs to develop a response.

I suggest the following as a good place to start:

Groothuis, Douglas. *Truth Decay: Defending Christianity Against the Challenges of Postmodernism*. Downers Grove, Ill.: InterVarsity Press, 2000.

Netland, Harold. *Encountering Religious Pluralism: The Challenge to Christian Faith and Mission*. Downers Grove, Ill.: InterVarsity Press, 2001.

Pearcey, Nancy. *Total Truth: Liberating Christianity from Its Cultural Captivity*. Wheaton, Ill.: Crossway, 2004.

Religion as illusion. Another challenge, not so common as the argument from evil, is that Christian faith is only an illusion. God did not make us in his image; we made him in ours. An excellent treatment of this will be found in Harvard psychologist Armand Nicholi's comparison of C. S. Lewis and Sigmund Freud:

Nicholi, Armand. *The Question of God: C. S. Lewis and Sigmund Freud Debate God, Love, Sex and the Meaning of Life*. New York: Free Press, 2002.

Doubt. Doubt is not so much an objection to Christian faith as a condition of the soul. Sometimes all arguments for Christian faith seem pallid compared to one's deep reservations. Then it is that you may need to address the root of these reservations. For that, I suggest three superb analyses:

Clark, Kelly James. *When Faith Is Not Enough.* Grand Rapids, Mich.: Eerdmans, 1997.

Guinness, Os. *God in the Dark: The Assurance of Faith Beyond a Shadow of a Doubt.* Wheaton, Ill.: Crossway, 1996.

Lewis, C. S. *A Grief Observed.* London: Faber and Faber, 1961.

A READING PLAN

An apologist for the Christian faith must not stop reading. Perpetual education should, in fact, be the norm for all Christians. Why not commit yourself to a few simple principles?

First, maintain a rich devotional life of Bible study and prayer.

Second, always have at least one book at hand at each of the places in your home (maybe your office too!) where you spend a lot of time. An attractive book may tempt you not to turn on the TV even for your favorite program. There are some temptations to which one should yield.

Third, discuss what you are reading with a friend and invite them to read the same book.

None of the books that I have mentioned above is beyond the ability of normally intelligent readers to understand. Most of them are great reads. There is, in fact, usually no reason to read a dull book. Well-written books exist in almost every area of value to maturing Christian apologists. But if you have reached this far in this book, you know that already.

If you would like to see an expanded annotated list of works on apologetics, you can find one in my book *Why Good Arguments Often Fail.*[4]

On your trip through the Bible and the great works of Christian thought . . .

Bon voyage!

Varna University, Bulgaria, April 1998

FINDING A VENUE for the propagation of the gospel in Bulgaria, by the time of this story, had become difficult. When I first visited Sofia in April 1991, Christian students secured a lecture room in the Klimint Ohridski University for my public lecture. I also spoke in the surgical theater of the Medical School, and I was a guest lecturer in a philosophy class as well. By October, when I made my second visit, the Bulgarian Orthodox Church was reacting to the influx of hundreds of evangelists from a wide spectrum of religions—evangelical Christian to Jehovah's Witnesses and Mormons to Eastern groups such as the Hare Krishnas. Getting the ear of the governing authorities, the Orthodox Church began preventing all other religious groups from easily securing a place to meet regularly or to sponsor lectures. By 1998 public venues had been unavailable for some time. All faiths other than Orthodox were being banned in Bulgaria.

In April 1998, when I returned for the third time, my lectures in Sofia had to be held in local churches, with the result that few people other than believers attended. In Varna, however, the case was different. My lecture was promoted as solely academic. "Relativism and Absolute Truth: I'm Okay. You're Okay. And That's Okay" was the published title. There are two main universities in Varna. When one of them discovered that the best lecture hall in the other university had been scheduled for the lecture, folks from the slighted one said, "Why didn't you ask us? We would have loved to host the lecture." Apparently the title was intriguing, and officials in the second university felt their institution had lost an opportunity to shine a bit brighter in the academic sun.

But there was a price to pay for this venue. I was asked to—and did—refrain from any direct promotion of Christian faith. I merely challenged the idea that any of six types of relativism could adequately account for the reality of religious claims. If any particular religion—Christianity, Hinduism, Buddhism—was right about God or the afterlife, then the others had to be wrong.

The lecture drew 150 people. About half, I am told, were probably not Christians, and a half-dozen were university professors. The professors asked excellent questions in the formal question-and-answer period. Then private conversations followed.

One young woman who talked to me said she felt that a divine power of some kind must exist, but she couldn't say much about it. I told her she was certainly right about her "feeling." Her sense of divine presence, I said, was put there by God, and it even had a name, *sensus divinitatus*. I encouraged her to follow through on that basic sense, to keep searching to know God better.

She also saw that the various notions of life after death could not all be true. "But," she asked, "which one is? And how can I know?" I suggested that she listen to what a man who had come back from the dead had himself said, and to do so that she read the Gospels. She was reluctant, but I insisted that she needed more information before she could decide. Then I directed her to the local IFES staff member and made sure that they both knew how to keep in touch. The Holy Spirit could not and still cannot be banned in Bulgaria.

The Call to Apologetics

MY WIFE MARJORIE has actually sung in Carnegie Hall. She hates it when I tell people that, but it's true. She is a lover of music and has sung in choirs since she was a young girl. She is not a soloist, but her sweet, clear alto voice is a credit to every group from trios to concert choirs. For thirty years she sang in the Downers Grove Oratorio Society, founded by Thelma Milnes, mother of Sherrill Milnes, who for a couple of decades was a lead baritone with New York City's Metropolitan Opera Company.

Over the years, Sherrill Milnes has supported his hometown oratorio society and has occasionally conducted its performance of Mendelssohn's *Elijah*. A few years ago he arranged for a performance of this oratorio at Carnegie Hall and invited the Downers Grove society to add its voices to a much larger chorus. So there I sat in the audience of this famous concert hall, glorying in this great piece of music, proud to hear Marjorie sing in the performance of her life.

"How do you get to Carnegie Hall?" begins the very old joke. "Practice, practice, practice." And, of course, being in the right place at the right time.

A PATH TO APOLOGETICS

About fifteen years ago, as I reflected on where I had just been and what I had just been able to do, I marveled. How does a kid born on a ranch in Nebraska, educated for six years in a one-room country schoolhouse with a different high-school-graduate teacher each year, get to lecture on the Christian implications of the work of Stanislav Lem, a Polish atheist science-fiction writer, to Irish students in the Samuel Beckett Room of Trinity College, Dublin?

It doesn't happen overnight. And the likelihood of its ever happening boggles my mind. I was never good at statistics anyway. If there is any principle to be drawn from this, it is a very simple one: If you devote your life to Christ and seek and do his will, you will be amazed at what transpires. Perhaps a few details of just how I came to give that lecture will illustrate this principle further.

My family moved twenty miles from our ranch to the tiny village of Butte, Nebraska, when I was about to enter the seventh grade. Sometime during the summer I committed my life to Christ and began to grow as a Christian. It was not long before I was convinced that I should do what I could to bring others to Christ, something I found both intimidating and hard to do. In college I became involved with InterVarsity Christian Fellowship and began leading evangelistic Bible studies and running the booktable for the IV chapter at the University of Nebraska. That's where I met my wife, a graduate student two years ahead of me academically. We both graduated in 1955, she with an M.A. in zoology, I with a B.A. in chemistry and English. I was commissioned as a second lieutenant in the U.S. Army the same day. The next day we were married.

After two years in the military, sixteen months of which were spent in postwar Korea, I studied English at Washington State College (now University), where Marjorie had been working as a genetics research assistant in the Agronomy Department. A year later I received an M.A. in English, we had our first child, and we immediately moved to the University of Missouri, where I continued English studies. During the year at Pullman, Washington, I was a volunteer worker with the local InterVarsity group. When I arrived in Columbia, Missouri, I immediately became the faculty adviser of its tiny, struggling InterVarsity chapter. Six years later, I received a Ph.D. in English (with secondary work in philosophy). During this time I taught a college Sunday school class and lectured occasionally for the local InterVarsity group, but never with any success in even garnering an audience, let alone in producing converts.

During my four years at Nebraska Wesleyan University, I occasionally spoke for the InterVarsity group at the University of Nebraska and tried but failed to get a faculty Bible study going at my own school. Then I was invited to become the first full-fledged editor at InterVarsity Press. This took me from Lincoln, Nebraska, to a suburb of Chicago, from the world of English literature to the world of Christian publishing. Here I expected to get lots of invitations to speak on a variety of campuses. Few came. Worse, when they did come and I went, very few students came to my lectures. It looked to me as if God was calling me to be an apologist behind the scenes, promoting as an editor the more effective work of others.

Then came an invitation to give a single lecture on worldviews— though I don't think we called them that—at an InterVarsity summer project at Cedar Campus. The next year I was invited to expand that lecture into six. One year later, Steve Board, one of the leaders of the project, encouraged me to put these lectures into print. They became *The Universe Next Door* (InterVarsity Press, 1976) which, though not written as a textbook, was immediately adopted by Christians teaching introduction to philosophy and religion at a host of Christian and secular universities. From that came invitations to lecture on university campuses and the beginning of a ministry that I had long wanted. More significant, for the first time students—both believers and seekers—came to the lectures. *The Universe Next Door* thus became the launching pad for my apologetics work. Other books followed, some like this one, born out of practice, practice, practice.

There is little specifically to be made from this autobiography. Budding apologists have asked me how they could "get my job." I tell them, "You can't. The process will probably never be repeated." After all, what sense would it make for me to tell them to get a Ph.D. in English literature? What I can say, though, is this: Seek first the kingdom of God, live under the lordship of Jesus Christ, practice, practice, practice, and you will be well on your way. You may never lecture in the Samuel Beckett Room at Trinity College, but you will find the audience God has in mind for you.

APOLOGETICS AND THE PROFESSIONS

There is, perhaps, one more point that can be made from my own experience. That is that God can use your talents, your gift and passion for apologetics, in ways that tie into so-called secular professions. As an English teacher, I was always aware of the Christian implications of the literature I taught—how it often presented the Christian faith, often found it wanting, promoted alternate views of reality and, if taken as a guide to life, led readers into despair. Teaching survey courses in world literature and English literature let me learn and take students through over two thousand years of intellectual history as well as literary history. Apologetics was a subtext of all literature courses I taught.

Only because of this could I even hope to speak on Stanislav Lem to Irish students and be both appropriately scholarly and intelligently Christian. My studies in literature and philosophy equipped me to lecture in Eastern European universities after the Berlin Wall came down in 1989. I gave the first lecture sponsored by a Christian group at the University of Sofia in Bulgaria in the philosophy department and taught in one of the classes as well.

One of the most exciting of these European venues was the Nansen Dialogue Center in Podgorica, Montenegro, in 2003. This center is sponsored by a Norwegian-based organization promoting reconciliation among contending political and ethnic peoples. I spoke, through a professional interpreter, on the flow of intellectual history from the Enlightenment age to postmodern times. The room was small but packed. No one responded with questions or comments. So I briefly told the story of how Albert Camus, realizing the inadequacy of his own existential philosophy, came as a seeker to a Methodist minister, Howard Mumma, and in the summer before he died made a profession of faith and sought baptism. This was a story that had just been published, and it stirred up a great deal of interest and disbelief.[1] It gave me the opportunity to answer questions that took the group deeply into the specifics of the Christian faith. It also offended a journalist, probably an atheist, who gave the lecture the worst newspaper review any of my talks (so far as I know) has ever received. That review prompted other journalists to come to my defense. The controversy went on for several days in the papers.

Most of my talks in North American and European universities have been sponsored by local groups of Christians, usually those affiliated with InterVarsity Christian Fellowship and the International Fellowship of Evangelical Students. In other words, I have my audience handed to me. I have never hung out a shingle that said, "Lecture at 4 p.m. Y'all come!" Rather the audience was found by *The Universe Next Door.*

I suppose there is a principle here. Publish a book that sells well! No, not really. That's not the principle. The principle is far simpler: Seek first the kingdom of God, and practice, practice, practice.

THE CALL OF GOD

In none of his lists of spiritual gifts does the apostle Paul mention "apologetics" or "defense of the faith." But "evangelists" are listed as gifts to the church in Ephesians 4:11, and that surely includes those evangelists who are spiritually skilled to present the Christian faith in a winsomely reasonable way. But how do Christians know that they are called to this special ministry? First, consider what constitutes any call.

It is an awesome thing to be called by God. Isaiah, struck by a vision of God, convicted of the profound depths of his and his nation's sin, purified by a burning coal placed on his lips by a seraph, heard the voice of God. "Whom shall I send?" God asked. And Isaiah replied, "Here am I; send me!" And God did, outlining the awesome task of bringing the terrible news of divine judgment (Is 6:1-13). Isaiah obeyed and over many years brought the news both good and bad as God revealed it to him. Despite his youth, Jeremiah too accepted God's call to "go to all to whom I send you, and . . . speak whatever I command you" (Jer 1:4-10). As a child, Samuel, under the tutelage of the prophet Eli, learned to hear God's voice, and as he grew up, "the LORD was with him and let none of his words fall to the ground" (1 Sam 3:19). These were all calls to follow God in the life of a prophet.

To read these Old Testament accounts with the eyes of the heart is to experience at least a shadow of the reality of an awesome God who is both utterly transcendent and beyond comprehension and who yet stoops to speak to his human creation, to call them to his service and equip them to be effective. This pattern continues in the New Testament, where again there is an almost impenetrable mystery. There sits Matthew minding his Roman business, collecting taxes. Jesus comes ambling by, spies Matthew and says, "Follow me." And Matthew just plain gets up and follows him—no questions asked (Mt 9:9). Peter, James and John get a lesson in fishing before Jesus calls them (Lk 5:1-11). These were calls to follow God in the life of a disciple and an apostle.

Indeed, the call of God comes in many ways to all sorts of people of all ages. In every case it is a call to follow God. But what about the call of God today? How do these biblical events relate to God's relationship with his people now? In Old Testament times God called his people through the prophets who spoke God's word into their present historical reality. He called Bezalel and his coworkers to construct the tent of meeting (Ex 31:1), for example. In the New Testament he called his followers first and foremost through Jesus Christ and then through the apostles. In post–New Testament times he has done so through the testimony of the biblical writers who give witness to Jesus—the Word made flesh, the very embodiment of God. We, then, must listen to the voice of God in Scripture. It is from our hearing of the Word of God that we will hear the call of God to us.

CALLING DEFINED

The biblical concept of God's call is far richer than I will be able to examine in depth here.[2] But in *The Call* Os Guinness has distilled from Scripture a definition that will serve our purpose well:

> *Calling is the truth that God calls us to himself so decisively that everything we are, everything we do, and everything we have is invested with a special devotion, dynamism, and direction lived out as a response to his summons and service.*[3]

The primary characteristics of God's call are threefold: it is *from* him, *to* him and *for* him. The call is not from the church, say, to come and do something religious. It is not from society, urging us to "do something about our poor schools or the violence on our streets." It is from God himself—the infinite-personal Lord of the universe, the God of the ages, the risen Christ.

Nor is the call first and foremost to some task that we are to perform or some function we are to fulfill in our religious community, in the world at large or even in the economy of God's kingdom. It is to God himself. The call is Person to person, so that the person in response can be intimately engaged with the Person. God calls us— each and every one of us—to himself.

Finally, the call is not primarily for ourselves or for others. If we hear and follow, there will indeed be marvelously positive effects on us and others, but the main goal is elsewhere. "The chief end" of our lives is "to glorify God," as the Shorter Catechism says. Guinness puts it this way: "*A life lived listening to the decisive call of God is a life lived before one audience that trumps all others—the Audience of One.*"[4]

The extent of the call is universal. The call of God engages every aspect of our life—who we are, what we think and what we do. And it does so with "devotion, dynamism and direction." Rather than throwing up our hands as we confront a confused and violent world, rather than giving up and stoically resigning ourselves to chaos, we live our lives with solid purpose. We may not know precisely where we are going in the next few days and weeks and years, but we know where we will end up, for we are seeking first the kingdom of God, and we know all that we really need will be added unto us.

When we think about a call to apologetics, we need to do so within the context of this all-encompassing vision, a vision that acknowledges that God is the Lord of the universe, the Lord of every single atom and every single person. "There is not one square inch of the entire creation about which Jesus Christ does not cry out 'This is mine! This belongs to me!'" said Abraham Kuyper.[5] Nothing short of our total commitment to the call of God brings him adequate honor.

THE CALL TO APOLOGETICS

It is important to realize from the outset that the call to apologetics is not a call to a particular job or career. It might work out that this is what will happen. You may find yourself playing that particular role as a "professional" employee of a church or other Christian ministry. But your call will not be first and foremost to a paid position with the business card reading "Professional apologist—all conversations turned to defense of the Christian faith." Your call is less specific, more generic, more a vocation or avocation than a profession.

I have never been one to think in terms of "career planning," attempting to envision just where I would like to be in five, ten, fifteen years and beyond. But when I look back, I can see patterns that have emerged. I have concluded, for example, that though I have been a university English professor, an editor, a traveling lecturer and an adjunct philosophy and theology teacher, none of these has been my vocation. What has tied all of these together is my vocation as a Christian witness to the intellectual world. This is very close, of course, to saying *apologist* to the intellectual world.

The call to apologetics, therefore, is a call to focus much of your Bible study, your prayer and your reading of books and magazines (Christian and not) on issues that relate most to those with whom you live and work and worship. You will be readying yourself to give a relevant defense of the faith in your particular niche of society.

VOCATIONAL REQUIREMENTS

There are two perspectives from which to discern one's vocation. The first is to recognize the characteristics that are necessary for a successful exercise of the vocation. The second is to identify your own specific talents and spiritual gifts and consider whether they are likely to equip you for such a vocation. In practice these two perspectives intertwine, as the above autobiography illustrates. But here I will separate them for purposes of analysis.

What then are the requirements for success as an apologist? There are, I believe, five basic requirements of equal importance: (1) a fascination with and delight in the intellectual life, (2) a passion for what can be learned from the Bible, (3) a life characterized by consistent holiness, (4) a love for people and (5) a growing ability to communicate with them on a profoundly personal level. All five requirements are wrapped up in what it means to be a Christian intellectual. In *Habits of the Mind* I listed the characteristics of such a person this way:

> An *intellectual* is one who loves ideas, is dedicated to clarifying them, developing them, criticizing them, turning them over and over, seeing their implications, stacking them atop one another, arranging them, sitting silent while new ideas pop up and old ones seem to rearrange themselves, playing with them, punning with their terminology, laughing at them, watching them clash, picking up the pieces, starting over, judging them, withholding judgment about them, changing them, bringing them into contact with their counterparts in other systems of thought, inviting them to dine and have a ball but also suiting them for service in workaday life.
>
> A *Christian intellectual* is all of the above to the glory of God.[6]

While this definition may sound as if it is more appropriate to a professor in the humanities, it fits the ordinary apologist as well. If one is to be a *Christian* apologist, every general characteristic of an intellectual must be turned toward the glory of God. Four special Christian intellectual virtues are required: a passion for truth, a passion for holiness, a passion for consistency and a compassion for others. The following list, adapted from Jay Woods, *Epistemology:*

Becoming Intellectually Virtuous, should lend clarity here.[7]

Acquisition Virtues: Passion for the Truth
inquisitiveness
teachableness
persistence
humility

Maintenance Virtues: Passion for Consistency
perseverance
courage
constancy
tenacity
patience
humility

Application Virtues: Passion for Holiness
love for God and his holiness
will to do what one knows
fortitude
integrity
humility

Communication Virtues: Compassion for Others
a passion for teaching
patience with difficult students
clarity of expression
orderliness of presentation
aptness of illustration
humility

There is not space enough here to look at each of these virtues in detail.[8] But I do want to single out several. And I want to address readers directly here.

First, notice that humility appears in each of the categories of intellectual virtues. If you are highly endowed with intellectual ability, this may be the hardest one for you to exhibit in practice! But for Christians it is one of the most important. More arguments may be lost by arrogance than are ever lost by poor reasoning. The reason should be obvious. Humility itself is a central virtue in Christian faith. If you show off your intelligence or your vast store of relevant information, you will lose the very ground on which rational thought rests—the ability to recognize the strength of an argument in light of its weaknesses. There are very few "knock-down" arguments for anything. Even if you have one, air it in such a way that the skeptic's dignity is not lost. This is especially important in dialogues where others are listening. Making a fool out of your opponent in public is a sure way to erect a barrier to his or her agreement with you.[9]

Second, you must have a humble passion for truth. This means that you must be ready to accept the truth wherever it is found—especially when it comes from the ones with whom you are speaking. An apologist who does not learn something from a dialogue with a nonbeliever is one who is not listening. At the least you will be learning what does and doesn't impress the skeptic. At most you may learn something even about the Bible or your own theological tradition that you didn't know before.

Third, you must have or develop an ability to think well—to recognize, construct, critique and recast arguments. Of course, a passion for truth will drive you to throw away any bad arguments you may be tempted to use. It will also drive you to constant reading and study. There is always another book or article to read, always more to learn from Scripture, always more to learn about the current culture—its contributions and distortions of the truth. An apologist who hates reading and despises scholarship is a contradiction in terms.

Fourth, you must have a passion for holiness. My guess is that the second most telling reason people fail to pay attention to the gospel is the way Christians live. Hypocrisy is a major barrier to belief— often listed by non-Christians as a major reason that they remain outside the faith. No Christian should be hypocritical, of course, but it is especially important for apologists.

Fifth, you must love people and love to be with people. If you are interested only in abstract arguments for the Christian faith and not in the people around, you may be called to be a scholar whose work aids apologists, but you may not be called to apologetics or to be an apologist as such. Moreover, if you are shy or fearful of contact with skeptics, you will have to overcome these obstacles or find another way to serve God.

Sixth, you must develop a growing ability to communicate deep spiritual truths at a profoundly personal level. Reason, as I have said over and over already, is not enough. It must be cloaked in rhetoric— convincing communication. This entire book has been as much about rhetoric as about reason. I hope I have been illustrating this combination by the very way in which I have cast the argument.

It should be obvious from the above that a Christian vocation of apologist will demand lots of so-called natural intellectual talent. But it will also require at least one spiritual gift.

SPIRITUAL REQUIREMENTS

Spiritual gifts are those special abilities with which God has endowed each of his children so that they might find and fulfill their mission. They enable each person to become who God wants each one to be.

So what spiritual gift, if any, is vital to a life of Christian apologetics? Most talents and spiritual gifts can find a place in apologetics. And though the New Testament does not list it, apologetics might well be one of them. But of the various spiritual gifts mentioned in the New Testament, the one that is central to apologetic life is the gift of *teaching* (Rom 12:7; 1 Cor 12:8, 29; Eph 4:11). A second relevant gift is *evangelism*.

Theologian Edmund P. Clowney lists several qualities that accompany teaching. First, "the teacher is a workman."[10] That means that he or she is diligent at the job. Indeed, a gifted teacher loves teaching and does not have to be goaded by a guilty conscience into working hard.

Second, the teacher brings out of his or her treasure "what is new and what is old" (Mt 13:52).[11] Research is necessary to constantly keep up with cultural shifts, new challenges to Christian faith, and changes in the temperament and character of people as society moves from baby boomers to generations X, Y, Z and who knows what else. Biblical scholarship—both critical and supportive—never ceases to emerge from the scholarly world. Those with the gift of teaching have the ability to absorb important information, place it in its context and use it wisely in constructing, using and revising arguments.

Third, a gifted teacher "can apply God's Word to the needs of the hearers with all longsuffering and teaching" (see 2 Tim 4:2).[12] In the pastorate, which is Clowney's main focus, the application is obvious. It is just as relevant in apologetics.

The second relevant gift of the Spirit is *evangelism*. I list this gift second, because, so it seems to me, effective apologetics is primarily focused on clearing away objections to Christian faith and presenting a winsome and reasonable positive case for its truth. In many cases apologetics is preevangelistic; it precedes evangelism by laying a foundation for a personal commitment to Christ. Of course, when the two gifts of teaching and evangelism are combined, the apologist becomes an evangelist.

After I became a Christian as an adolescent, I soon came to believe that evangelism was a Christian's main task. I regretted that I was never very effective in my attempts. In college I led evangelistic Bible studies in my dorm room. To the best of my knowledge, none of my non-Christian friends became believers. And for that matter, most of those who have become Christians partly through my apologetic efforts have not done so in my presence. Nor have, again so far as I know, any of them become believers solely through my books or talks. One told me that he had been reading Francis A. Schaeffer but was not convinced; then he found *The Universe Next Door* in a city library, read that and became a Christian. Then there was the Christian who took her boyfriend to one of my talks in Prague. Several months later, through her influence and reading Scripture, he became a believer, and he refers back to my lecture as a key element in his conversion. He went on to study theology. A university student from a Sikh family attributes her conversion in part to hearing for the first time that people should hold their religious beliefs "because they are true." This is a key point in my lecture discussion "Why Should Anyone Believe Anything at All?" She then became an active evangelist in her university.

At least once, however, a person became a Christian in my presence, even though I didn't know it was happening. At Indiana University, my student hosts told me that there would be a skeptic at my lecture who would ask all kinds of tough questions. In the event, however, no one asked much of anything at all. The talk, I thought, fell on deaf ears. But afterward, when I mentioned my disappointment to my host, she said, "What do you mean nothing happened? John [not his real name] became a Christian." He had simply sat qui-

etly and, as I spoke, moved from doubt to faith; in the weeks to come
he became a vibrant Christian.

Sometimes I learn about people coming to faith years later. For example, just before I stepped to the lectern at Claremont College in
California, a young woman hurried across the auditorium and said,
"Remember me? I transferred here from Colby College in Maine,
where you spoke two years ago. I wanted to tell you that three students became Christians after your lecture there! That's why I'm excited about tonight."

Everyone is responsible for being a witness to Christ, but not
everyone is given either the special spiritual gifts of teaching or evangelism. I believe that I have been given a much larger measure of the
first of these gifts than of the second.

DISCERNING ONE'S OWN CALL

How do you stack up with the above characteristics of an apologist?
If you have the passions requisite to being an apologist, how well are
they growing in you a sense of God's call? In my own case, in my
youth and even my middle years I could not have foreseen where I
would be at age seventy. I rather doubt that anyone can do this—even
if they seek God's help in trying. What is important is that at each
step along the way you are following Jesus as best you know how. He
will take care of the rest.

The passions for truth, holiness, people and communication come
first. But they may not be rooted in reality. For a reality check, there
are some helps along the way—the judgment of your close Christian
friends, the sense of your pastor (if he or she knows you well), the
results of your academic work (you should do fairly well in your formal studies in the Bible, theology, philosophy and any other humanities and social science courses you have taken), the comments of

your teachers (Christian and not) and the pleasure you have taken (or pain you have experienced) in your apologetic endeavors so far.

One type of test for an apologetics call I would caution against: any test that would attempt to evaluate your temperament or personality. I have known effective apologists of every stripe—the jolly and the morose, the stiffly formal and the hang-loose, the arcane scientist who writes only for fellow scientists and the clever philosopher who presents his case in witty dialogues, the silver-tongued and the plain-spoken.

Finally, there is the test of practice, practice, practice. If doing apologetics—not just the study of apologetic arguments—begins to become second nature and you just can't stop doing it . . . well, that should clinch the argument. Doing will become knowing.

Notes

Preface

[1] I am, of course, describing a presentation by Francis A. Schaeffer, who in the 1960s was ministering first to students who heard about L'Abri, his home and retreat center in Switzerland. The earliest statements of his apologetics are to be found in *Escape from Reason* (Downers Grove, Ill.: InterVarsity Press, 1968) and *The God Who Is There* (Downers Grove, Ill: InterVarsity Press, 1968).

[2] The theologian was Thomas J. J. Altizer, the historian John Warwick Montgomery. See *The Altizer-Montgomery Debate* (Downers Grove, Ill.: InterVarsity Press, 1969).

[3] The scholar was C. S. Lewis, the book *Mere Christianity* (New York: Macmillan, 1952), a compilation of three slim volumes that were issued earlier.

[4] The cleric was John R. W. Stott, the rector of All Souls Church in London; the book was *Basic Christianity* (Downers Grove, Ill.: InterVarsity Press, 1958).

Chapter 1: What Is Apologetics?

[1] Ronald B. Mayers, for example, defines apologetics as "a philosophical, theological and historical demonstration of the truthfulness of Christianity," to show that Christianity has a distinctive view of all of reality, and to refute alternate, conflicting views (*Both/And: A Balanced Apologetic* [Chicago: Moody Press, 1984], pp. 7-10).

[2] William Edgar writes, "If we accept the preliminary definition of apologetics as sound argument, we see all of Scripture testifying to the need for apologetics" (*Reasons of the Heart: Recovering Christian Persuasion* [Grand Rapids, Mich.: Baker, 1996], p. 43). Edgar does a stellar job of showing how the Bible—from start to finish—engages in apologetics (see esp. pp. 33-50).

[3] See Alan M. Stibbs, *The First Epistle General of Peter*, Tyndale New Testament Commentary (Grand Rapids, Mich.: Eerdmans, 1959), pp. 49-58.

[4] The apostle Peter does not outline the course such a defense should take, but Eckhard J. Schnabel shows how his letter contains comments on and allusions to a wide

range of notions that should be included in such a defense: "The term *apologia* signifies that they should be prepared to give an account of the objective foundation of their Christian faith and identity. For example, they should be prepared to explain that sins can be forgiven because the Father of Jesus Christ is merciful and because Jesus has died and has been raised from the dead (1 Pet 1:3). They should be able to explain that Christians have the hope of life after death, when they will receive 'an inheritance that is imperishable, undefiled, and unfading' (1 Pet 1:4). They should be willing to speak of their experience of the power of God in their everyday life, which enables them to endure the hostility and opposition that they encounter (1 Pet 1:5-6). They should be willing and able to speak of Jesus Christ, whom they have not seen but still love, not least because he gives them 'an indescribable and glorious joy' (1 Pet 1:8). They should be able to explain the grace that God offers when Jesus is revealed (1 Pet 1:13). They should be able to explain why they have been saved through the 'precious blood of Christ,' who died on the cross (1 Pet 1:18-19). They should be able to explain why the world, which has a beginning, will come to an end (1 Pet 1:20). They should be able to explain their faith in the God who raised Jesus from the dead and soon will raise all people from the dead (1 Pet 1:21). They should be able to explain the meaning of the 'new birth' that they have experienced, and the meaning of the 'living word of God' that they have heard and in which they are instructed in their weekly meetings (1 Pet 1:23-25)" (*Early Christian Mission*, vol. 2, *Paul and the Early Church* [Downers Grove, Ill.: InterVarsity Press, 2004], pp. 1524-25).

[5]I have examined this lecture in more depth in *Why Good Arguments Often Fail* (Downers Grove. Ill.: InterVarsity Press, 2006), pp. 129-45.

[6]Of course, Athens too was filled with immorality, but the people Paul was addressing there were intellectuals. Had he been addressing the bulk of the Athenians in the marketplace, he might well have been less distinctly intellectual and more broadly relational.

[7]Jude addresses the same problem in the opening to his letter: "Certain intruders" have come into the church and are perverting "the grace of our God into licentiousness" and denying "our only Master and Lord Jesus Christ" (v. 4). So Jude calls on the faithful to "contend for the faith" (v. 3).

[8]As I was finishing work on this book, I accidentally ran across a quotation from Presbyterian theologian John Oman. It so paralleled my definition that I thought it worth

quoting here: "There is only one right way of asking men to believe, which is to put before them what they ought to believe because it is true; and there is only one right way of persuading, which is to present what is true in such a way that nothing will prevent it from being seen except the desire to abide in darkness; and there is only one further way of helping them, which is to point out what they are cherishing that is opposed to faith. When all this has been done, it is still necessary to recognize that faith is God's gift, not our handiwork, of His manifestation of the truth by life, not our demonstration by argument or of our impressing by eloquence" (John Oman, *Grace and Personality* [New York: Association Press, 1961), p. 121, as quoted by Martin E. Marty, *Varieties of Unbelief* [New York: Image, 1966], pp. 198-99).

Chapter 2: The Value of Apologetics

[1]The basic organization for this and the following chapter is based on a list of values and limits of apologetics prepared by Dan Denk, staff member of InterVarsity Christian Fellowship and fellow laborer in the field of apologetics; the commentary on this list is my own.

[2]In a review of Colin McGinn's *The Making of a Philosopher: My Journey Through Twentieth-Century Philosophy* (New York: HarperCollins, 2002), J. B. Stump notes that "Bertrand Russell's influence was . . . evident in the eradication of religion from McGinn's life. For although he did not come from a religious family McGinn considered himself a Christian believer for a time during his youth. But Russell 'extinguished the last remnants of religiosity from my soul' (35). 'Religion simply lost its grip on me after a couple of years of fairly fervent belief. I shed it like an old skin; it slid off me quite naturally and painlessly' (36)" (*Christian Scholar's Review,* Summer 2004, p. 606). We can well ponder what might have been the effect had McGinn, while his faith was ebbing away, encountered a credible apologetic for the Christian faith. We do know that the ontological argument, while intriguing, has not persuaded him: Stump writes, "He is still fascinated with the ontological argument for God's existence as a kind of logical exercise (contra the usual critique of the argument, he claims that existence can be a predicate), but he remains thoroughly naturalistic in his ontology" (p. 606).

Chapter 3: The Limits of Apologetics

[1]Thomas V. Morris, ed., *God and the Philosophers: The Reconciliation of Faith and Reason*

(New York: Oxford University Press, 1994), and Kelly James Clark, *Philosophers Who Believe* (Downers Grove, Ill.: InterVarsity Press, 1993).

[2]Thomas V. Morris, "Suspicions of Something More," in *God and the Philosophers*, p. 16.

[3]C. Stephen Layman, "Faith Has Its Reasons," in *God and the Philosophers*, p. 92.

[4]Ibid., p. 93.

[5]David Downing makes a convincing case for this in *Into the Region of Awe: Mysticism in C. S. Lewis* (Downers Grove, Ill.: InterVarsity Press, 2005).

[6]Morris, "Suspicions of Something More," pp. 17-18.

[7]Nancy Pearcey, *Total Truth: Liberating Christianity from Its Cultural Captivity* (Wheaton, Ill.: Crossway, 2004), p. 54.

[8]Ibid., p. 55.

[9]An ancient Chinese philosopher once said, "Once I, Chuang Chou, dreamed that I was a butterfly and was happy as a butterfly. I was conscious that I was quite pleased with myself, I did not know that I was Chou. Suddenly I awoke, and there I was, visibly Chou. I do not know whether it was Chou dreaming that he was a butterfly or the butterfly dreaming that it was Chou" (from *A Source Book in Chinese Philosophy*, trans. and ed. Wing-Tsit Chan [Princeton, N.J.: Princeton University Press, 1963], p. 190).

[10]In case anyone is thinking that this is cheating, a type of bait-and-switch technique, remember this: Scripture itself—without any scholarly comment—is the most powerful testifier to its own veracity that there is. It is, after all, "sharper than any two-edged sword." It divides "soul from spirit" (Heb 4:12)! If we point people to the Scripture and let it do its job, we may not have to argue for its historical reliability. Or when we do argue for its reliability, we may find our arguments succeeding.

[11]Roy Clouser, *Knowing with the Heart: Religious Experience and Belief in God* (Downers Grove, Ill.: InterVarsity Press, 1999), p. 156; see also p. 118.

[12]I have addressed this issue in *Why Should Anyone Believe Anything at All?* (Downers Grove, Ill.: InterVarsity Press, 1997), and in chaps. 8 and 11 of *Why Good Arguments Often Fail* (Downers Grove, Ill.: InterVarsity Press, 2006).

[13]C. S. Lewis, *Surprised by Joy* (London: Geoffrey Bles, 1955), p. 233.

[14]Clouser, *Knowing with the Heart*, p. 62.

[15]Gary Habermas surveys the various ways the *witness of the Holy Spirit* has been understood in relation to the assurance of salvation and to apologetic arguments, and he offers his own assessment. See his "The Personal Testimony of the Holy Spirit to

the Believer and Christian Apologetics," *Journal of Christian Apologetics,* Summer 1997, pp. 49-64.

[16]I am especially impressed with John G. Stackhouse's description of the apologetic task and have stolen his title for a piece of my own: *Humble Apologetics: Defending the Faith Today* (New York: Oxford University Press, 2002).

Chapter 4: The Contexts of Apologetics

[1]You can find excellent examples of how questions can be answered well in two essays in J. Budziszewski, "Practical Responses to Relativism and Postmodernism," parts 1-2, and R. Douglas Geivett, "Can a Good God Allow Evil and Suffering?" in *Philosophy: Christian Perspectives for the New Millennium,* ed. Paul Copan, Scott B. Luley and Stan W. Wallace (Addison, Tex.: CLM and RZIM, 2003), pp. 89-121, 122-48.

[2]Geivett, "Can a Good God Allow Evil and Suffering?" pp. 129-32.

[3]Max Scheler (1824-1928) turns out to be a significant philosopher who gets half a column in the 882-page *Cambridge Dictionary of Philosophy* (Cambridge: Cambridge University Press, 1995), p. 714; Plato gets four pages, Kant five.

[4]Christian philosopher Alvin Plantinga confesses that the existence of great evil in the world "remains deeply baffling" ("A Christian Life Partly Lived," in *Philosophers Who Believe* [Downers Grove, Ill.: InterVarsity Press, 1993], p. 69). This he says after writing two books on the problem of evil and arguing that if you believe that there is great evil in the world, that very fact is a "powerful theistic argument from evil" that God exists (ibid. pp. 69-72). Ralph C. Wood in "Ivan Karamazov's Mistake," *First Things,* December 2002, pp. 29-36, shows how Feodor Dostoyevsky in *The Brothers Karamazov* gives no intellectual answer to the problem of evil but rather shows how two characters, Father Zosima and Alyosha, answer with "deeds rather than reasons." My own response to the problem of evil can be found in my *Why Should Anyone Believe Anything at All?* (Downers Grove, Ill.: InterVarsity Press, 1994), pp. 180-89.

[5]Rebecca Manley Pippert, *Out of the Saltshaker,* 2nd ed. (Downers Grove, Ill.: InterVarsity Press, 1999), pp. 89-91. Roy Clouser recommends something very similar. See his comments quoted on pp. 44-45.

[6]John G. Stackhouse and David K. Clark agree (see John G. Stackhouse Jr., *Humble Apologetics: Defending the Faith Today* [New York: Oxford University Press, 2002],

p. 202; and David K. Clark, *Dialogical Apologetics: A Person-Centered Approach to Christian Defense* [Grand Rapids, Mich.: Baker, 1993], p. 223). But I learned this firsthand some fifty years ago when I sold a set of aluminum pots and pans to the young woman who overheard my pitch to her friend. Her friend declined.

Chapter 5: The Arguments of Apologetics

[1]James W. Sire, *Why Should Anyone Believe Anything at All?* (Downers Grove, Ill.: InterVarsity Press, 1997), pp. 180-89.

[2]Richard Dawkins, *The Blind Watchmaker* (New York: W. W. Norton, 1988), p. 6.

[3]Richard Dawkins made this frequently quoted (and criticized) statement in a book review in the *New York Times,* April 9, 1989. His rejoinder criticism can be found in "Ignorance Is No Crime," *Free Inquiry Magazine* 21, no. 3, or at <www.secular humanism.org/library/fi/dawkins_21_3.html>. He comments, "Of course it *sounds* arrogant, but undisguised clarity is easily mistaken for arrogance. Examine the statement carefully and it turns out to be moderate, almost self-evidently true." Dawkins then explains how it is "moderate," in the process adding "tormented, bullied and brainwashed" into the mix of causes for not believing the evolutionary story. The notion, however, that his outrageous statement is "almost self-evidently true" illustrates the power of Dawkins's own commitment to the evolutionary theory; it does not show the statement to be "almost self-evidently true," nor does the remainder of his essay "Ignorance Is No Crime."

[4]James W. Sire, *Why Good Arguments Often Fail* (Downers Grove, Ill.: InterVarsity Press, 2006), pp. 156-85.

Chapter 6: The Call to Apologetics

[1]Howard Mumma, *Albert Camus and the Minister* (Brewster, Mass.: Paraclete, 2000).

[2]I commend to readers three books I have found very helpful in writing this chapter: Os Guinness, *The Call: Finding and Fulfilling the Central Purpose of Your Life* (Nashville: Word, 1998); Edmund P. Clowney, *Called to the Ministry* (Phillipsburg, N.J.: Presbyterian & Reformed, 1964); and Gordon Smith, *Courage and Calling* (Downers Grove, Ill.: InterVarsity Press, 1999).

[3]Guinness, *Call,* p. 29.

[4]Ibid., p. 73.

[5]Abraham Kuyper, quoted by ibid., p. 165.

[6]James W. Sire, *Habits of the Mind* (Downers Grove, Ill.: InterVarsity Press, 2000), pp. 27-28.

[7]W. Jay Wood, *Epistemology: Becoming Intellectually Virtuous* (Downers Grove, Ill.: InterVarsity Press, 1998), pp. 34-40. My list is not an exact duplicate (I have added some and omitted others he includes).

[8]For more detail on these virtues, see Wood, *Epistemology,* and Sire, *Habits of the Mind,* esp. pp. 106-25.

[9]See Scott R. Burson and Jerry Walls's fascinating analysis of the tension in the apologetics of both Francis Schaeffer and C. S. Lewis between overconfidence in the power of arguments to arrive at certain truth and recognition of the fallibility of the arguer due to the effects of the Fall: *C. S. Lewis and Francis A. Schaeffer: Lessons for a New Century from the Most Influential Apologists of Our Time* (Downers Grove, Ill.: InterVarsity Press, 1998), pp. 239-44. Also see my own *Why Good Arguments Often Fail* (Downers Grove, Ill.: InterVarsity Press, 2005), pp. 73-79.

[10]Ibid.

[11]Ibid., p. 65.

[12]Ibid.

Index